We live in a fallen world. It leads to life in tension, and sometimes a life full of stress. Stephen Hiemstra takes us on a needed tour of the kind of character it takes to face such a life. His careful look at the Beatitudes through the portrait of life in tension frees us to reflect God well in a world full of need. Read this book and be better equipped to face life as it is.

Dr. Darrell L. Bock
Executive Director for Cultural Engagement, Howard G. Hendricks Center for Christian Leadership and Cultural Engagement and Senior Research Professor of New Testament Studies, Dallas Theological Seminary
Dallas, Texas

Stephen Hiemstra's Life in Tension reminds me of Bonhoeffer's Cost of Discipleship, because it is an earnest, personal effort to hear and follow the voice of Jesus here and now. Hiemstra was a professional economist but is also trained in reformed theology, and thus he speaks as one whose feet are on the ground and who has walked some of the walk and has stumbled along the way. Unlike Bonhoeffer, though, Hiemstra knows his hearers are not deeply familiar with the Sermon on the Mount. Yet his book, too, is for people who know from experience what Luther meant by "sin boldly but believe more boldly."

Jonathan Jenkins
Pastor, Klingerstown Lutheran Parish
Klingerstown, Pennsylvania

We don't often think of our life as one lived in tension, but as believers that's exactly how we live. Stephen Hiemstra's Life in Tension takes us through the Beatitudes and provides a blueprint for Christians to navigate this tension with ourselves, with the world and with Christ. Each chapter ends with a prayer and reflective questions designed to draw the reader into deeper contemplation of this tension. For those seeking answers on how to live a life in tension, this is the book for you.

Sarah Hamaker
Author of *Ending Sibling Rivalry: Moving Your Kids From War to Peace*
Fairfax, Virginia

The Christian life is filled with tension, paradox, and upside down requisites for obedience to the biblical text and the clarion call of God. Life in Tension provides a solid, biblical theology for how God invites us to reflect his priorities in this life. With the Beatitudes as our faithful guide, Hiemstra unpacks Jesus' loving intentions for all of his disciples. Follow along and you'll discover the abundant life.

Dr. Stephen Macchia
Founder and President of Leadership Transformations,
Director of the Pierce Center for Disciple-Building at Gordon-Conwell Theological Seminary, Author of ten books, including *Becoming a Healthy Church* (Baker), *Crafting a Rule of Life* (IVP), and *Broken and Whole* (IVP)
South Hamilton, Massachusetts

A thorough examination of Bible verses given the three tensions that we, as human beings, are confronted with. The soul reflection—within ourselves, with others, and with our almighty creator God, helps the reader to take ownership of their spiritual journey, and empowers healing through forgiveness and biblical reflection.

Sam Lee
Manassas, Virginia

Also by Stephen W. Hiemstra:

A Christian Guide to Spirituality

Una Guía Cristiana a la Espiritualidad

LIFE IN TENSION

Forgotten Path in Winter

LIFE IN TENSION

Reflections on the Beatitudes

Stephen W. Hiemstra

T2Pneuma Publishers LLC
Centreville, Virginia

LIFE IN TENSION: *Reflections on the Beatitudes*

T2Pneuma Publishers LLC, P.O. Box 230564, Centreville, Virginia 20120
http://www.T2Pneuma.com

The image on the front covers is a scene of the passion of Christ called *The Way to the Calvary* and is a wooden carving from a church in Santiago de Compostela, Alameda, Spain. The electronic image is licensed from iStockPhoto (http://www.iStockPhoto.com) of Cagary in Alberta, Canada.

Cover and layout designed by SWH

Publisher's Cataloging-in-Publication (Provided by Quality Books, Inc.)
    Hiemstra, Stephen W., author.
      Life in tension : reflections on the Beatitudes /
      Stephen W. Hiemstra.
      pages cm
      Includes bibliographical references and index.
      LCCN 2015921089
      ISBN 978-1942199045 (paperback)
      ISBN 978-1942199052 (Kindle)
      1. Beatitudes--Criticism, interpretation, etc. 2. Spiritual life--Christianity. 3. Values--Religious aspects--Christianity. 4. Stress (Psychology)--Religious aspects--Christianity. I. Title.
      BT382.H546 2016   226.9'306   QBI16-900036

FOREWORD

By Nathanael Snow[1]

*J*esus dwelt among us to live a life of holiness, to forgive sins through his death and resurrection, and to establish a new kingdom, which is his church. The church is composed of individuals from every tribe and nation as a new organic entity, indwelt by the Holy Spirit, with a peculiar identity and ethic. The relationship between Christ and his church, described by the Apostle Paul as the bride of Christ, remains a great mystery (Eph 5:32).

Early in his ministry, Jesus' disciples misunderstood his role. He was a healer, prophet, and teacher, but few thought of him as the Son of God (Matt 16:16). And none expected his brand of messiah.

For the attentive disciple, Jesus' role and teaching was plainly described in the Sermon on the Mount. But go easy on the disciples for their ignorance—Jesus' sermon, an ordination service for disciples, is still misunderstood. Consider the Beatitudes:

> *Honored are the poor in spirit, for theirs is the kingdom of heaven.*

---

1 Former missionary to Durham, NC, Assistant Professor of Economics, Indiana Wesleyan University.

Honored are those who mourn, for they shall be comforted.

Honored are the meek, for they shall inherit the earth.

Honored are those who hunger and thirst for righteousness, for they shall be satisfied.

Honored are the merciful, for they shall receive mercy.

Honored are the pure in heart, for they shall see God.

Honored are the peacemakers, for they shall be called sons of God.

Honored are those who are persecuted for righteousness' sake, for theirs is the kingdom of heaven.

Honored are you when others revile you and persecute you and utter all kinds of evil against you falsely on my account. (Matt 5:3–12)

For a biblically challenged generation like ours, the Beatitudes still read like code. Yet, as Stephen Hiemstra explains, Jesus cast a new vision, a new identity, which calls his disciples out of the crowds to sit as his feet as he teaches. They are to be honored, not maligned, for being poor in spirit, prone to mourn, meek, hungry for righteousness, merciful, pure, peaceful, persecuted, and reviled. They are to be honored, not maligned, for their wounds place them in the company of prophets (Matt 5:12).

Perhaps the disciples misunderstood because he was talking to the crowd or to a unborn generation. But, as Hiemstra explains, disciples then and disciples now have no excuse. The Beatitudes provide the key to the code, a hermeneutic, a way of reading the Old Testament that reveals God's eternal plan for his kingdom (Matt 5:17). In fulfilling scripture, Jesus boldly declares a simple truth: God keeps his promises—we should too.

Yet, we have trouble believing it. No one wants to be meek or poor in spirit; no one wants to make God's peace; no one wants mercy or to offer it; no one wants to receive persecution graciously. These responses require regeneration—a higher calling, and a greater expectation than our nature allows. But, in Christ, our fallen nature is restored; we are a new creation (2 Cor 5:17).

In Christ, though I am at war with myself, Jesus loves me as I am. Though I hide from God, Jesus seeks me out, clothes me with righteousness, and ushers me into the Father's presence. Though I resent my neighbors, Jesus loves them. The relationship gaps within ourselves, with God, and with our neighbors cause tension. Yet, in Christ and through the indwelling of the Holy Spirit, God sovereignly dispenses his grace and heals our wounds, narrowing the gaps and relieving the tension.

Still, sanctification requires a lifetime of faithful devotion because our minds require reminders and our hearts require comfort. Through prayer we remain in Christ and through meditation we internalize God's truth. This devotional offers direction for our footsteps and prayer for the journey.

Come and join disciples from every tribe and nation who sit at Jesus' feet, learning who we are, and who we are becoming. Receive the blessings; pray without ceasing; linger in God's grace. Embrace a life in tension; or, as Stephen suggests, hear the master's words; walk in his footsteps; and experience Christian joy!

PREFACE

Be holy because I am holy (Lev 11:44) says the Lord God.

W hen God enters our lives, we change. This change occurs as we increasingly reflect Christ's divine image
in our lives and the Holy Spirit works in our hearts and minds
as we behold him (2 Cor 3:16–18). The Apostle Paul calls this
process sanctification (Rom 6:19), which means that we accept
Christ's invitation to a lifelong journey to become more holy—
sacred and set apart—and the Holy Spirit's guidance along the
way. As Christ's church—the called out ones,[1] our sanctification
is a group activity and, like any activity where individuals travel
at their own pace, tension among believers is expected.

Tension? What tension? Sanctification is necessary because we sin. Sin separates us from other people, from God, and
from the person that God created us to be. Sanctification presumably reduces our sin, encourages us to abide in union with
God[2] and draw closer to the person that God created us to be,
but it also widens the gap between us and those resisting the

---

1 The word for church in Greek is ekklesia (ἐκκλησία) which means ones
called out (1 Cor 1:2).

2 Hickman (2016, 104–124) observes that abiding in union with God requires that we become comfortable with doing nothing to earn God's grace,
pray simply knowing that God knows our thoughts), staying attentive to God's
work in our lives, and being led to follow as God leads. Still, we are prone to
strive rather than to rest in God's love.

Holy Spirit (1 Thess 5:19).[3] Consequently, sin and sanctification can both potentially tense up all three relationships.

Tension comes up daily, as a pastor observes:

> *Would you drink from a dirty cup?[4] No—of course not. If you were given a dirty cup, you would refuse the cup and ask for another.[5]*

Someone accustomed to clean cups immediately recognizes a dirty one.[6] When we model our lives after Christ, we reveal our identity as Christians; we are set apart from those around us in tension with the world. As conscious image bearers, we naturally begin to share in the tension that exists between God and this world, which implies that *how we live and how we die matters to God.*

This tension that we feel is a subjective mirror image to three gaps that we can objectively describe. The first gap is within each of us and it describes the distance between our natural selves and the person who God created us to be.[7] This gap can

---

3 Niebuhr (2001, 39) writes: *"In his single-minded direction toward God, Christ leads men [and women] away from the temporality and pluralism of culture."*

4 See: 2 Tim 2:20.

5 Pastor Anthony K. Bones of African Gospel Church of Nairobi, Kenya (http://AGCKenya.org) speaking at Trinity Presbyterian Church, Herndon, Virginia on January 14, 2015.

6 Here we are defining tension. How this tension gets resolved is also interesting. In the dirty cup analogy, do we reject the dirty cup or quietly wash it ourselves so as not to embarrass our host?

7 The Apostle Paul writes: *"For I do not understand my own actions. For I do not do what I want, but I do the very thing I hate."* (Rom 7:15)

lead to humiliation in the eyes of the world and shame within us, as we realize how far we have fallen from God's image for us. The second is gap is between us and others[8] can lead to isolation, ridicule, and persecution, as we can no longer run with the crowd or accept its norms. The third is the gap between us and God created by sin[9] can lead to feelings of fear, abandonment, and a loss of spiritual power, as we realize what it means to live without God's presence and blessings.

Can you feel the tension created by these gaps—the shame, the isolation, and the fear? Can you imagine being persecuted for your beliefs? Are you okay with it or do you try to run away? *How do we respond creatively to this tension?*

Alone with these three gaps, we are lost; but in Christ we are never alone. Christ works in our lives to close these gaps through his reconciling example in life, his atoning work on the cross and his enabling gift of the Holy Spirit. The Holy Spirit enables us by grace through faith to participate actively in our

---

8 "The LORD said to Cain, *why are you angry, and why has your face fallen? If you do well, will you not be accepted? And if you do not do well, sin is crouching at the door. Its desire is for you, but you must rule over it.' Cain spoke to Abel his brother. And when they were in the field, Cain rose up against his brother Abel and killed him.*" (Gen 4:6–8)

9 The Prophet Isaiah writes: *Woe is me! For I am lost; for I am a man of unclean lips, and I dwell in the midst of a people of unclean lips; for my eyes have seen the King, the LORD of hosts!*" (Isa 6:5)

own sanctification while experiencing God's peace in the midst of life's tensions.

Early in his ministry, Jesus preached a sermon, a kind of commissioning service for his disciples. He advised his disciples to be humble, mourn, be meek, chase after righteousness, be merciful, be holy, make peace, be persecuted for the right reasons, and wear persecution as a badge of honor (Matt 5:1–11). Incredibly, in the middle of this sermon and in spite of expected opposition, Jesus says:

> You are the light of the world. A city set on a hill cannot be hidden. Nor do people light a lamp and put it under a basket, but on a stand, and it gives light to all in the house. In the same way, let your light shine before others, so that they may see your good works and give glory to your Father who is in heaven. (Matt 5:14–16)

This parable about light offers two important insights for our understanding of tension. First, this passage makes no sense unless tension exists between darkness and light—light normally drives out darkness. Second, this passage alludes to the creation accounts where we read:

> The earth was without form and void, and darkness was over the face of the deep. . . . And God said, Let there be light, and there was light. And God saw that the light was good. And God separated the light from the darkness. (Gen 1:2–4)

Creation involved creating light. The implication is that Christians who embrace tension with the world are participating in a second creation (or re-creation) event (2 Cor 5:17).

Recognizing Christ's re-creative work in our lives, we participate through the power of the Holy Spirit, not only in our own sanctification, but in the sanctification of others. In other words, progress in reducing one gap in our lives affects the other two.[10] Attending to the sin in our lives, for example, makes it easier to get along with others and helps us to be more receptive to the Holy Spirit. Likewise, reducing our gap with God helps us appreciate God's love for those around us and sensitizes us to the corrupting power of sin in our own lives. In God's economy is nothing is wasted.

Structure of the book. In exploring the spiritual dimensions of tension in our lives, I reflect on the Beatitudes in Matthew's Gospel. The Beatitudes introduce Jesus' Sermon on the Mount and prioritize his teaching. Because the sermon serves as an ordination service for the disciples, the importance of the Beatitudes for the early church, Christian spirituality, and discipleship cannot be overstated.[11]

---

10 (Nouwen 1975, 15).

11 Guelich (1982, 14) citing Kissinger (1975) reports that: *"Matthew 5–7 [appears] more frequently than any other three chapters in the entire Bible in the Ante Nicene [early church] writings"*.

The chapters in this book divide into three parts: tension with ourselves (part A), tension with God (part B), and tension with others (part C). Each part contains three of the nine Beatitudes found in Matthew's Gospel (numbered from one to nine with decimal points identifying particular sections within them).

Four sections appear in each Beatitude. The first section focuses on understanding what Jesus said and how he explained it. The second section examines the Old Testament context for each Beatitude. The third section examines the New Testament context—how did the Apostles respond to and expand on Jesus' teaching? And the final section applies the Beatitude in a contemporary context and how we should respond. Each reflection is accompanied by a prayer and questions for further study.

Soli Deo Gloria.

Heavenly Father,

I believe in Jesus Christ, the son of the living God, who died for our sins and was raised from the dead. Come into my life, help me to renounce and grieve the sin in my life that separates me from God. Cleanse me of this sin, renew your Holy Spirit within me so that I will not sin any further. Bring saints and a faithful church into my life to keep me honest with myself and draw me closer to you. Break any chains that bind me to the past—be they pains or sorrows or grievous temptations, that I might freely welcome God, the Father, into my life, who through Christ Jesus can bridge any gap and heal any affliction, now and always. In Jesus' previous name, Amen.

ACKNOWLEDGMENTS

*I*n the fall of 2014, I was invited to speak at a local mosque about my book, *A Christian Guide to Spirituality*. Speaking at a mosque was new to me and anticipating this visit I spent three days fasting and praying for guidance. Instead of guidance on the mosque visit, God inspired me to write this book.

We never work in isolation. Without the support and encouragement of my editors, Reid Satterfield[1] and Nohemi Zerbi[2]—both also friends and pastors—this book might never have been written. Thank you.

Thanks also to my writing instructor, Mary J. Yerkes,[3] whose lectures and readings inspired a re-write and substantive edit of *Life in Tension* during the later stages of this project.

Life is not all work. I would like to thank my family, es-

---

1 Reid edited my first book, *A Christian Guide to Spirituality* (2014). Previously, Reid was a missionary for African Inland Mission and currently served as the Coordinator of Discipleship and Spiritual Formation at St. Patrick's Anglican Mission, Charlotte, NC. He also lecturers for Perspectives that provides churches with educational resources for engaging in world missions and provide spiritual direction to church leaders in and around the Charlotte Metro area.

2 Nohemi edited my previous book, *A Christian Guide to Spirituality*, in both the English (2014) and Spanish (2015) editions. She is a seminary student at University of Dubuque Theological Seminary and currently attends Faith Evangelical Presbyterian Church in Alexandria, VA.

3 Mary describes herself as: a professional writer, speaker, spiritual director, and seasoned mentor (http://www.MaryYerkes.com).

pecially my mom, for their constant encouragement and support when I was not as available, either in body or spirit, as I should have been. Thanks also to my friends in Christ at Centreville Presbyterian Church,[4] where I am an elder, and at Almuerzo para el Alma,[5] where I have volunteered on Wednesdays since July 2013.

4 http://www.CentrevillePres.com.

5 *Almuerzo para el Alma* is Spanish for *Luncheon for the Soul* which provides a meal and a service for day workers in Herndon, Virginia at Trinity Presbyterian Church (http://www.trinityherndon.org).

CONTENTS

FOREWORD...v

PREFACE...ix

ACKNOWLEDGMENTS.................................... xvii

INTRODUCTION

Gospel as Divine Template.. 2

Tension with Ourselves..7

Tension with God...12

Tension with Others...19

The Beatitudes.. 24

PART A: TENSION WITH OURSELVES

1. HONORED ARE THE POOR IN SPIRIT

1.1: Honored are the Poor in Spirit   34

1.2: Jesus' Mission Statement Gives Us Hope 39

1.3: Be Humble, Be Salt and Light   44

1:4: Living Out Poor in Spirit 49

2. HONORED ARE THOSE THAT MOURN

2.1: Joy in Sorrow   54

2.2: Lament over Sin   61

2.3: Death Means Resurrection   67

2.4: Grief Builds Character, Defines Identity 71

3. HONORED ARE THE MEEK

3.1: Resolve Tension into Identity   78

3.2: Meekness Speaks Volumes   83

3.3: Meek is the Pastoral Gene90

3.4: Lead Out of Meekness   94

PART B: TENSION WITH GOD

4. HONORED ARE THOSE THAT HUNGER AND THIRST

4.1: Jesus: Passionately Seek the Kingdom of God............ 102
4.2: Hunger and Thirst for God.....................................107
4.3: Fools for Christ.. 112
4.4: In Jesus Completeness is Restord.......................... 118

5. HONORED ARE THE MERCIFUL

5.1: Show Mercy, Receive Mercy............................... 122
5.2: God's Core Values... 127
5.3: Mercy as a Path to Salvation............................... 132
5.4: Jesus Models Image Ethics.................................. 136

6. HONORED ARE THE PURE IN HEART

6.1: Be Holy For I am Holy...................................... 142
6.2: A Right Spirit and Clean Heart............................ 147
6.3: Prune, Intensify, and Apply.................................152
6.4: Living into Our Call.. 157

PART C: TENSION WITH OTHERS

7. HONORED ARE THE PEACEMAKERS

7.1: Make Peace—Embody Shalom............................ 168
7.2: Prince of Peace...173
7.3: Trinity of Peace... 179
7.4: Peace on God's Terms..186

8. HONORED ARE THE PERSECUTED

8.1: Promote Righteousness...................................... 192
8.2: Righteous Suffering...196
8.3: Christian Paradox.. 202
8.4: Bless Those that Persecute.................................. 206

9. HONORED ARE THE REVILED

9.1: Persecution Gets Personal.................................... 212
9.2: Suffering Often Predates Salvation...........................218
9.3: Persecution Can Be Transformative....................... 223
9.4: Persecution and Lethargy.................................... 229

CONCLUSIONS

Surprising Priorities... 238
Spiritual Links and Tensions.....................................243
The Road Ahead...248

REFERENCES.. 253
SCRIPTURAL INDEX.. 263
ABOUT THE AUTHOR.. 271
AFTERWORD.. 273

INTRODUCTION

GOSPEL AS DIVINE TEMPLATE

TENSION WITHIN OURSELVES

TENSION WITH GOD

TENSION WITH OTHERS

THE BEAUTITUDES

Gospel as Divine Template

if you confess with your mouth that Jesus is Lord and believe in your heart that God raised him from the dead, you will be saved. (Rom 10:9)

C hristianity began in a graveyard with the resurrection (Ps 16:10). The resurrection could not have occurred without Jesus' crucifixion and death which was, in turn, associated with his life and ministry. Because Jesus' life and ministry was chronicled looking back from the resurrection, each sentence in the New Testament should be prefaced with these words: *Jesus rose from the dead, therefore* . . . Jesus' life, ministry, suffering, death, and resurrection are the Gospel story.[1]

Just before his death the Apostle Paul writes from prison:

> *that I may know him and the power of his resurrection, and may share his sufferings, becoming like him in his death, that by any means possible I may attain the resurrection from the dead.* (Phil 3:10–11)

In other words, the Jesus story—life, ministry, suffering, death, and resurrection—was for Paul a template for the Christian journey of faith, beginning with the end in mind. Yet, we know that the end of the story—like its beginning—is in Christ and pro-

---

1 After the Gospels themselves, consider, for example, the sermons by both Peter (Acts 2:14–41; 10:34–43) and Paul (Acts 13:16–41) which focus on Jesus' life story.

vides Christian hope (1 Pet 1:3).[2]

While our eyes remain on *the prize* (Phil 3:14) and our expectations for the end times, our relationship with each member of the Trinity sustains us day to day. The Holy Spirit is with us, empowers us, and helps us to break the power of sin. Jesus Christ's life and ministry models a faithful life in a stressful world. God Our Father demonstrates love, grace, and sovereignty over all earthly powers. Because of God's sovereign power and presence, our future hope of the resurrection becomes our present hope in Christ (Col 1:24).

The resurrection accordingly influenced how early Christians read the Beatitudes, as in: *Jesus rose from the dead, therefore "Honored are the poor in spirit, for theirs is the kingdom of heaven."* (Matt 5:3) Notice that the Beatitude explicitly refers to the kingdom of heaven—a place of healing and rest where the resurrected are assumed to go. Because early Christians read this Beatitude in view of the resurrection, so should postmoderns.[3]

2 Smith (2006, 29–30) sees the church as a place where the Gospel is not intellectualized but rather lived out (incarnate). It is a place where the story of Jesus is told and retold. He writes: *"The church is the site where God renews and transforms us—a place where the practices of being the body of Christ form us into the image of the Son."* (30). These practices include the sacraments, Christian marriage and child-rearing, radical friendship, and learning patience.

3 The postmodern period can be dated from the fall of the Berlin Wall in 1989 because as the threat of communism receded, western culture turned increasingly inward and away from its Christian heritage. In particular, while moderns believe in one objective truth, postmoderns do not. Likewise, while moderns believe in separation of church and state, postmoderns prefer per-

More typically, postmoderns read the Beatitudes as *"pie in the sky"*—unobtainable and unrealistic. But how much risk is there in buying a stock if you already have tomorrow's stock report? If tomorrow's paper eliminates today's risk, why dawdle in buying the stock? Unobtainable and unrealistic goals suddenly become reasonable— in light of the resurrection common fishermen become extraordinary apostles.

Knowing that the end of the story is in Christ, the Beatitudes outline the three tensions in our spiritual life: our inward tension with ourselves (poor in spirit, mourning, and meekness), our upward tension with God (righteous, merciful, and pure), and our outward tension with the world (peacemakers, persecuted, and reviled).[1] Inward tension exists, but we know the Holy Spirit will guide us. Upward tension exists, but we know that God loves us. Outward tension exists, but we have Christ's example in seeking reconciliation and an open door to the future (Rev 3:20).[2]

Because of our reconciliation with God, we know that our sinful nature which drives this tension was not part of God's

sonal freedom to the exclusion of church involvement in questions of morality, especially as it pertains to gender roles.

1 Nouwen (1975, 15) observes that we move from loneliness to solitude in our inner life; we move from illusion to prayer in our life with Christ, and we move from hostility to hospitality in our communal life.

2 *"God's primary will for your life is not the achievements you accrue; it's the person you become."* (Ortberg 2015, 15).

original design. Breaking God's design, sin emerged in the Garden of Eden as Adam and Eve turned away from God and allowed sin to enter their lives (Gen 3:6). Yet, even as sin entered the world and tensed up our lives, God provided for our restoration through the death and resurrection of Jesus Christ (Gen 3:15).

Jesus rose from the dead, therefore our faith starts with God, not with us.

Almighty Father, Beloved Son, Ever-present Spirit,
We give thanks for the work of Jesus Christ, who lived, ministered, suffered, died, and rose from the dead that the Gospel might live in us. May we know him and his power; share in his suffering and his death; that we might also be resurrected with him into new life (Phil 3:10–11). Break the power of sin in us; empower us to live in reconciliation to one another; and grant us words to lift up in prayer all the days of our lives. In Jesus' precious name, Amen.

＊

Questions
1. Where did Christianity begin and why do we care?
2. What is the *"Gospel template"* and what are its components?
3. What was the focus of early Christian preaching?
4. How should we read the New Testament?
5. What are the sources of tension with ourselves, with others, and with God?
6. How does the resurrection affect Christian living?

Tension with Ourselves

For I do not understand my own actions. For I do not do what I want, but I do the very thing I hate. (Rom 7:15)

*W*e are the best fed and most pampered generation of all time; yet, our young people and senior citizens are committing suicide at historically high rates and *"ordinary children today are more fearful than psychiatric patients were in the 1950s."* (Lucado 2012, 5) Why?

One answer is that we have become painfully isolated from ourselves: *"We live in a society in which loneliness has become one of the most painful human wounds"* (Nouwen 2010, 89). Our isolation has been magnified by a loss of faith and community, leaving us vulnerable to anxiety and depression.

Isolated people often ruminate about the past. In ruminating, obsessing about a personal slight, real or imaged, amplifying small insults into big ones. For psychiatric patients who are not good at distinguishing reality and illusion, constant internal repetition of even small personal slights is not only amplified, it is also remembered as a separate event. Through this process of amplification and separation, a single spanking at age 8 could by age 20 grow into a memory of daily beatings.

Amplified in this way, rumination absorbs the time and

energy normally focused on meeting daily challenges and planning for the future. By interfering with normal activities, reflection, and relationships, rumination slows normal emotional and relational development and the ruminator becomes increasingly isolated from themselves, from God, and from those around them.

Why do we care? We care because everyone ruminates and technology leads us to ruminate more than other generations. The ever-present earphone with music, the television always on, the constant texting, the video game played every waking hour, and the work that we never set aside all function like rumination to keep dreary thoughts from entering our heads.[1] Much like addicts, we are distracted every waking hour from processing normal emotions and we become anxious and annoyed[2] when we are forced to tune into our own lives. Rumination, stress addiction[3], and other obsessions have become mainstream lifestyles that leave us fearful when alone and in today's

1 Technology connects us yes, but it more often isolates us from one another. A "Facebook friend", for example, is denied a vote if you get tired of them and remove them as a friend. Real friends give us immediate feedback and require explanations. For an exhaustive treatment, see: (Turkle 2011).

2 This is a form of escalation in which psychiatric patients amplify rather than dissipate any tension in conversation. Even polite disagreement quickly evokes an increasingly hostile response.

3 Stress addiction is a situation in which stress becomes the norm in our lives. Peace and quiet upset us because we are unaccustomed to it. Because we cannot relax, stress threatens not only our mental well-being, but also our physical health.

society we are frequently alone even in the company of others.[4] We are in tension with ourselves.

Jesus sees our tension and offers to relieve it, saying:

> *Come to me, all who labor and are heavy laden, and I will give you rest. Take my yoke upon you, and learn from me, for I am gentle and lowly in heart, and you will find rest for your souls. For my yoke is easy, and my burden is light.* (Matt 11:28–30)

Self-centered rumination is a heavy burden, not a light one, and Jesus models the Sabbath rest, prayer, and forgiveness that break rumination by encouraging us to look outside ourselves. In Sabbath rest we look outside ourselves to share in God's peace, to reflect on Christ's forgiveness, and to accept the Holy Spirit's invitation to prayer. In prayer we commune with God where our wounds can be healed, our strength restored, and our eyes opened to our sin, brokenness, and need for forgiveness. When we sense our need for forgiveness, we also see our need to forgive. In forgiveness, we value relationships above our own personal needs which break the cycle of sin and retaliation in our relationships with others and, by emulating Jesus Christ, we draw closer to God in our faith.

---

4 Loneliness in the company others is the theme of a recent book by Sherry Turkle (2011). Nouwen (1975, 25) sees loneliness as related more to addiction than to rumination. Blackaby (2014, 47) talks about getting stuck in a particularly sad or particularly happy season of life.

Faith, discipleship, and ministry require that we give up obsessing with ourselves. On our own, our obsessions are too strong and we cannot come to faith, grow in our faith, or participate in ministry. For most people, faith comes through prayer, reading scripture, and involvement in the church, all inspired by the Holy Spirit. For the original apostles, the discipling was done by Jesus himself.

In the Beatitudes, Jesus tutors the disciples and says that we will be honored in at least three ways:

> *Honored are the poor in spirit, for theirs is the kingdom of heaven. Honored are those who mourn, for they shall be comforted. Honored are the meek, for they shall inherit the earth.* (Matt 5:3–5)

Jesus takes the world's threats to our identity, self-worth, and personal dignity and reframes them as promises that we will receive the kingdom of heaven, be comforted, and inherit the earth. But, Jesus ties these promises to discipleship and does not extended them to spectators.1

---

1 The yoke (Matt 11:28–30) Jesus uses to describe the work of a disciples was a leather collar worn by a work animal, such as a horse, to allow them to bear the burden of the work without injury. Disciples bear the yoke of discipleship; spectators do not. This implies that the blessings of Jesus are available exclusively to disciples. This is what James, Jesus' brother, means when he says: *"But be doers of the word, and not hearers only, deceiving yourselves."* (Jas 1:22)

Father God,

We thank you for your willingness to break into our little worlds. Break our obsession with ourselves—the person that we know so well, but have trouble being truthful to. Shine your light into the darkness; drive the cloud of despair away; help us to accept your Gospel by engaging it, living it, and sharing it. Bridge the gap between our false selves and our true selves in Christ; bridge the gap between us and others; bridge the gap between us and you. By the power of your Holy Spirit, re-create us again as whole people. In Jesus' precious name, Amen.

Questions
1. What is ironic about our situation as the best fed generation to walk the face of the earth?
2. How does author, Henry Nouwen, interpret this irony?
3. What is rumination and why do we care?
4. What are three things that Jesus models which break rumination and why are they important?
5. What is the focus of the first three Beatitudes?

Tension with God

Saul, Saul, why are you persecuting me? And he said, Who are you, Lord? And he said, I am Jesus, whom you are persecuting. (Acts 9:4–5)

*T*he idea of tension with God surprises many Christians for at least three reasons. The first reason is that the church's focus on the humanity of Christ and off of the divinity of Christ cloaks the urgings of the Holy Spirit leaving us ignorant of our distance from God. The second reason is that a focus on conversion and off of sanctification—the process of nurturing our faith—leaves us living secular lifestyles ignorant of God's will for our lives. A final reason is that indifference to sin blinds us to our true selves in Christ, to our neighbors, and to God.

It is not an accident that each of these three reasons is highly theological because postmoderns mostly avoid theology—a fourth reason which may be why tension with God may come as a surprise. The postmodern focus on the emotional content of faith and off of the implications of these three theological trends hides our tension with God and quietly robs our faith of its power.[1] Oblivious to the tension, Christians are lulled into believing in a kind of tension-free, ersatz[2] Christianity that pro-

1 The Holy Spirit works a bit like electricity—we all know which vacuum cleaner is plugged in!

2 Ersatz means an inferior or fake substitute. Some people describe this as feel-good Christianity, which is less descriptive and has a more critical con-

vides individualized services[3] and generally promises to insulate them from the problems of life. When life's problems arise, their ersatz Christianity provides no substantive guidance for dealing with them, leading people to become angry with God, and leave the church. It is accordingly helpful to review the reasons that people are unaware of the tension between them and God.

Humanity versus Divinity of Christ. Our secular society questions Christ's divinity but has no problem with Jesus' humanity. If Christ is *only* human, then Jesus is no more than an interesting teacher, the church becomes another interest group, and conversion is as mundane as joining another club. If Christ is not divine, then Jesus' teaching has no claim on us[4] and we can simply ignore any tension with God that Jesus' teaching might signal.

Conversion versus Sanctification. Over the centuries, Christian leaders have debated the priority of conversion over sanctification. For example, Jonathan Edwards, often praised as the great American theologian, advocated that church members have a personal relationship with Jesus[5]—a fruit more of sanc-

---

notation.

3 More consumption activities (empathy, interesting worship, social activities), less theology, moral guidance, or service obligations.

4 This is not a trivial point. The Apostle Paul writes: *"if Christ has not been raised, your faith is futile and you are still in your sins."* (1 Cor 15:17)

5 Noll (2002, 45) writes: *"The dismissal occurred when Edwards abandoned*

tification than of conversion—only to have his Northampton church dismiss him in 1750. If sanctification can be thought of as a series of conversion experiences whose consequence is a closer relationship with God, then tension with God can be seen as a sign of progress in spiritual formation and maturity.

Think about the tension with God in the life of the Apostle Paul. When God told Ananias to go and baptize Saul, he questioned God's intentions:

> But the Lord said to him, Go, for he is a chosen instrument of mine to carry my name before the Gentiles and kings and the children of Israel. For I will show him how much he must suffer for the sake of my name. (Acts 9:15–16)

Paul was called as a Christian and an Apostle to the gentiles and to suffer for the Name. Do you think Paul's calling created tension in his life, with God, and with others? Paul himself described the life he gave up as a Rabbi and a Jew as rubbish (Phil 3:8) compared to what he gained as a believer. Still, he met every sort of affliction during his ministry[1] and struggled with

his grandfather Stoddard's practice of open communion and instead began to insist that candidates for church membership (and the privilege of communion) offer a convincing statement of saving faith".

1 "Are they servants of Christ? I am a better one—I am talking like a madman—with far greater labors, far more imprisonments, with countless beatings, and often near death. Five times I received at the hands of the Jews the forty lashes less one. Three times I was beaten with rods. Once I was stoned. Three times I was shipwrecked; a night and a day I was adrift at sea; on frequent journeys, in danger from rivers, danger from robbers, danger from my own people, danger from Gentiles, danger in the city, danger in the wilderness, danger at sea,

an unanswered prayer over a thorn in the flesh—a euphemism perhaps suggesting a grievous sin[2] over which he was not victorious (2 Cor 12:7).The point in this example is that if tension with God is a challenge even for the spirituality mature, then being unaware of our tension with God signals spiritual immaturity or, worse, spiritual lethargy.[3]

Ignorance of Sin. Spiritual lethargy starts with ignoring sin, which even a hardened atheist should worry about. Sin can be: doing evil (sin), breaking a law (transgression), or failing to do good (iniquity). Sin cuts us off from ourselves, from our neighbors and from God leading to tensions in all three dimensions. Ignoring sin is like driving too fast on an icy road or throwing dirty sand in your gas tank—it can hurt others and messes everything up, including our relationship with God.

God's forgiveness through Christ sets us right with God and relieves our guilt, but does not in most instances reverse the

---

danger from false brothers; in toil and hardship, through many a sleepless night, in hunger and thirst, often without food, in cold and exposure. And, apart from other things, there is the daily pressure on me of my anxiety for all the churches." (2 Cor 11:23–28)

2 Romans 7 focuses on the power of sin and seems too personal a discussion to have been completely vanquished in Paul or in any one of us.

3 Consider also the case of Job. Scripture describes Job as a man: *"blameless and upright, one who feared God and turned away from evil."* (Job 1:1) Still, God tells Satan: *"Behold, all that he [Job] has is in your hand. Only against him do not stretch out your hand."* (Job 1:12) Do you think that Job felt spiritual oppression? Do you think Satan's afflictions created tension between Job and God?

effects of sin on our person and on others. God can forgive the murderer, for example, but that does not bring the dead person back to life or relieve the perpetrator of punishment under law.

Tension with God is more critical than tension in a human relationship, because that our very existence depends on God.[1] Sin cuts us off from God, but when we avoid sin the channels of communication with God open and we can perceive the promptings of the Holy Spirit. When we obey the Spirit's promptings we join God in his ongoing creative work in the world and become more like Jesus, sanctified, which involves pain and sacrifice. In turn, our sacrifices signal to God, to those around us, and to ourselves that our transformation in Christ is real (2 Sam 24:21–25).

Jesus honors disciples who faithfully pursue godliness:[2]

> *Honored are those who hunger and thirst for righteousness, for they shall be satisfied. Honored are the merciful, for they shall receive mercy. Honored are the pure in heart, for they shall see God.* (Matt 5:6–8)

Notice that these Beatitudes mirror attributes that God uses to describe himself—"*merciful and gracious, slow to anger, and* abounding in *steadfast love and faithfulness*" (Exod 34:6)—and

---

1 Provoking tension with God makes about as much sense as a diver 300 feet under water discarding their air tank—life itself is threatened.

2 Fairbairn (2009, 67) reminds us not to dwell on causality here: "*Christianity teaches us that our significance does not ultimately lie in what we accomplish or what we do; it lies in the one to whom we belong.*" In this context, the Beatitudes outline the attributes of followers of Jesus, not a to-do list.

offer a key to growing as divine image bearers.

Father God,

Thank you for sending your son, Jesus Christ, into our lives to draw us closer to you. Save us from our own evil thoughts and feelings. Unstop our ears; open our eyes; and flood our hearts the promptings of your Holy Spirit. Forgive our sin; redeem us from our transgressions; and cleanse us from our iniquities. Give us a heart for your word and grant us the mind of Christ. Teach us to lean on your law and to share your grace that we might become true disciples: honored to hunger and thirst for your righteousness; honored to be merciful; honored to pursue Godliness. Through the power of the Holy Spirit and the grace available to us through Jesus Christ. In Jesus' precious name, Amen.

Questions

1. What are four reasons that tension with God is not obvious to many people? Do you agree?
2. What is ersatz Christianity and why do we care?
3. Why is the divinity of Christ important?

4. What is sanctification and why is it important?

5. What is spiritual oppression and who in the Bible suffered it?

6. What are three kinds of sin? Why do atheists need to worry about it as much as Christians?

7. Which three Beatitudes focus on the tension with God?

8. Some people distinguish practicing holiness (stop sinning) from pursuing godliness (doing good). What is the difference between them?

Tension with Others

You have heard that it was said, You shall love your neighbor and hate your enemy. But I say to you, Love your enemies and pray for those who persecute you, so that you may be sons of your Father who is in heaven. (Matt 5:43–45)

Whintersen we become Christians, tension with others can arise in two ways. First, when we draw closer to God, the gap between the biblical values we are growing into and the cultural values we are leaving behind widens, and people notice. After I started seminary, for example, I noticed that some of my saltier friends stopped using profanity in my presence. Second, because God loves people, when we draw closer to God and become more like Jesus, we cannot help but love people too.[1] Although sanctification creates a gap between us and others, God's love flowing through us works to bridge this gap.[2]

Consider the story of Abraham and his nephew, Lot. God blessed Abraham and then revealed plans to destroy two sinful cities, Sodom and Gomorrah (Gen 18:17–20). Set apart from the

---

[1] Love defines who God is: *"For God so loved the world, that he gave his only Son, that whoever believes in him should not perish but have eternal life."* (John 3:16) Love also defines the church, as Jesus commands: *"A new commandment I give to you, that you love one another: just as I have loved you, you also are to love one another. By this all people will know that you are my disciples, if you have love for one another."* (John 13:34–35) When we sacrificially love people outside the church, we participate with God in loving them.

[2] *"If a brother or sister is poorly clothed and lacking in daily food, and one of you says to them, Go in peace, be warmed and filled, without giving them the things needed for the body, what good is that?"* (Jas 2:15–16)

world, Abraham then prayed to God to spare the cities for the sake of the righteous living there (Gen 18:23–32), presumably including his nephew, Lot.

Lot showed no problem living in Sodom or compassion for his neighbors. Quite the contrary, Lot displayed bad judgment in choosing to live in Sodom (Gen 13:10) and only left Sodom on the urging of angels sent to retrieve him (Gen 19:16). Lot's wife found it even harder to leave Sodom and disobeyed the angels by looking back at the flaming city (Gen 19:26).

Reflecting on the destruction of Sodom and Gomorrah, the church can position itself relative to culture in three ways: working to redeem the culture like Abraham, inattentive to the culture like Lot, or beguiled by the culture like Lot's wife. Jesus commends Abraham's approach,[1] but the grace extended has limits, as Jesus instructs his disciples:

> And whatever town or village you enter, find out who is worthy in it and stay there until you depart. As you enter the house, greet it. And if the house is worthy, let your peace come upon it, but if it is not worthy, let your peace return to you. And if anyone will not receive you or listen to your words,

---

1 Luke writes: "And he sent messengers ahead of him, who went and entered a village of the Samaritans, to make preparations for him. But the people did not receive him, because his face was set toward Jerusalem. And when his disciples James and John saw it, they said, Lord, do you want us to tell fire to come down from heaven and consume them? But he turned and rebuked them. And they went on to another village." (Luke 9:52–56)

> *shake off the dust from your feet when you leave that house or town. Truly, I say to you, it will be more bearable on the day of judgment for the land of Sodom and Gomorrah than for that town.* (Matt 10:11–15)

The disciples are to offer peace (that is, to preach the Gospel) to everyone, but, for the sake of others willing to listen, those unwilling to listen have their wishes respected—*"shake off the dust from your feet"* (Matt 10:14).[2]

The gap between others and ourselves is the focus of the last three Beatitudes:

> *Honored are the peacemakers, for they shall be called sons of God. Honored are those who are persecuted for righteousness' sake, for theirs is the kingdom of heaven. Honored are you when others revile you and persecute you and utter all kinds of evil against you falsely on my account.* (Matt 5:9–11)

In these Beatitudes, Jesus neither denies, nor excuses, nor runs away from persecution. Instead, he treats persecution as a ministry opportunity—*"Love your enemies and pray for those who persecute you"* (Matt 5:44)—and he offers consolation for those suffering it. The implication is that tension with others is the norm, not the exception, for Christian disciples.

---

2 Also see: Mark 6:11, Luke 9:5, 10:11, and Acts 13:51. Also: Rom 1:28.

Almighty Father, Beloved Son, Holy Spirit,

We praise you for being willfully present in our lives—teach us to be willfully present in the lives of those around us. We confess our need for holiness—may your example shine through us. We confess that we are often attracted more to culture and less to you—teach use how to live faithfully in tension with the world around us. We confess the need to be reconciled with those that pain us and those we pain—teach us how to live sacrificially in your name. We thank you for the life and witness of your son, Jesus Christ, and for many spiritual gifts showered on us by your Holy Spirit. Grant us strength for the day, grace for those we meet, and peace. In Jesus' precious name, Amen.

Questions
1. What creates tension between us and others and what reduces it?
2. What three types of relationships between us and culture do we see in the story of Abraham and his family? What is a fourth possibility that we can see in the work of Christ?
3. What limits ministry to non-believers in the New Testament and why?

4. Which three Beatitudes deal with the tension with others?
5. What advice did Jesus offer for dealing with tension with others?

The Beatitudes

Serve the LORD with fear, and rejoice with trembling. Kiss the Son, lest he be angry, and you perish in the way, for his wrath is quickly kindled. Blessed are all who take refuge in him. (Ps 2:11–12)

*T*he Beatitudes poetically introduce Jesus' Sermon on the Mount (Matt 5–7), which sets priorities, redefines honor among disciples, and commissions his disciples. The sermon offers the lengthiest statement of Jesus' teaching and the early church cited it more frequently than any other passage in scripture.[1] As an introduction, the Beatitudes interpret the Old Testament in ways that surprised his disciples then and continue to surprise us now, suggesting that the Beatitudes desire careful study.

Gospel Context. In both Matthew and Luke, the Beatitudes appear immediately after Jesus calls his disciples[2] and addresses the disciples, serving as a preamble for the sermon that

---

1 Guelich (1982, 14) citing Kissinger (1975) reports that: *"Matthew 5–7 [appears] more frequently than any other three chapters in the entire Bible in the Ante Nicene [early church] writings".*

2 The calling of the disciples occurs in Luke 6:13–16 and Matt 4:18–22. The Beatitudes follow in Luke 6:20–26 and Matt 5:3–12. Before the sermon, Jesus is tempted in the desert, returns to Galilee after John's death, and begins his ministry by calling the apostles. Furthermore, Jesus' teaching in Matthew 4 sounds a bit like John the Baptist— *"Repent, for the kingdom of heaven is at hand."* (Matt 4:17)—and only three verses summarize Jesus' ministry after calling the disciples (Matt 4:23–25). This sequence of events in Matthew 4 suggests that the sermon occurs early in Jesus' ministry while Luke 6 suggests a later date which follows a series of Sabbath controversies, the last one being the healing of a man with a withered hand (Luke 6:7–11).

follows.

The sermon addresses the disciples personally, much like Jesus' earlier call to ministry—"*Follow me, and I will make you fishers of men.*" (Matt 4:19). This is not a passive call to be spectators, but an active call for disciples who will share in his suffering, at a time when the arrest and beheading of John (who baptized Jesus) was still fresh in their minds (Matt 4:12; 14:10).[3]

Suffering—extreme tension—is an obvious theme in the sermon both because of John's recent death and because of the ongoing threats to Jesus' life that began even before his birth (Matt 1:18–25; 2:1–13). Suffering, we learn in the Beatitudes, is part of being a faithful disciple and we know that the disciples got the message because ten out of the eleven faithful disciples died a martyr's death[4].

Literary Context. The Beatitudes take their name from the Latin translation (beati) of the Greek word for honor (μακάριος) which means "*humans privileged recipients of divine favor*" or "*favored, blessed, fortunate, happy, privileged*".[5] Jesus repeats μακάριος nine times.

---

3 Summarizing this point, Bonhoeffer (1995, 89) writes: "When Christ calls a man, he bids him to come and die."
4 Only the Apostle John avoided a violent death (Fox and Chadwick, 2001, 10).
5 (BDAG 4675, 2, 2a).

The Bible uses repetition for emphasis—twice is emphasis; three times is highly emphatic; and nine times is unprecedented. This emphatic repetition is reinforced by the sermon's content. The sermon in Matthew pictures Jesus as the new Moses issuing a new law of grace on a mountain (like Mount Sinai), while in Luke the sermon presents both blessings and curses (woes), a pattern associated with covenantal law (Deut 28). In other words, the literary style and content of the text are both attention-grabbers for a Jewish audience.

Old Testament Context. Jesus' repeated use of μακάριος in the sermon alludes to Psalm 1 in the Greek[1] translation, where it says:

> *Blessed is the man who walks not in the counsel of the wicked, nor stands in the way of sinners, nor sits in the seat of scoffers; but his delight is in the law of the LORD, and on his law he meditates day and night.* (Ps 1:1–2)

Psalm 1 pictures God's shalom, a call to holiness, and integration (the opposite of tension) within ourselves, with God (through obedience to the law), and with others with an amazing economy of words.

Other references to μακάριος speak, not of integration,

---

1 Most New Testament citations from the Old Testament come from the Greek translation, not the Hebrew, because both Jews and Gentiles, especially outside Israel, found Greek more familiar than Hebrew in the first century.

but of tension, such as political tension (Psalm 2) and affliction (Isaiah 30). In Isaiah 30, for example, God makes an interesting promise to those that wait for him:

> And though the Lord give you the bread of adversity and the water of affliction, yet your Teacher will not hide himself anymore, but your eyes shall see your Teacher. (Isa 30:20)

The teacher here is the Messiah who blesses those who suffer *"the bread of adversity and the water of affliction"*—a poetic phrase meaning persecution, while the word for teacher (מוֹרֶיךָ) also means early rain[2], a form of blessing in a desert region like Israel.

Commissioning Purpose. In his sermon, Jesus redefines the meaning of honor, an important, but neglected, translation of μακάριος (Neyrey 1998, 164).[3] This translation is important because the ancient world had an honor-shame culture where even a small insult requires an immediate and sometimes deadly response[4]—Jesus forbids such responses. When Jesus taught forgiveness, enemy love, and turning the other cheek, he radically confronted the honor-shame cultural norm, where masters had honor and slaves had mostly shame.

2 Interestingly, the Greek Old Testament does not use the word teacher at all, perhaps because this double meaning is absent in the Greek.

3 If Jesus had wanted to convey the idea of blessed, then the more conventional word in Greek would eulogetos (France 2007, 161).

4 A postmodern example of an honor-shame subculture can be seen when you hear news accounts about a young person being shot in a dispute over tennis shoes—a source of pride and a frequent marker for gang membership.

Dishonor in the ancient world Jesus redefined as honor among his disciples. Jesus said:

> *Honored are you when others revile you and persecute you and utter all kinds of evil against you falsely on my account. Rejoice and be glad, for your reward is great in heaven, for so they persecuted the prophets who were before you.* (Matt 5:11–12)

In other words, heavenly rewards follow from earthly persecution. In a culture obsessed with glory and honor—especially family honor, the preferred translation for μακάριος here is honor, not blessing, because it is more consistent with the rest of Jesus' sermon and the cultural context of the ancient world.[1]

Lord of Lords, Prince of Peace, Spirit of Holiness,

We praise you for blessing us with life, a vision of how to live it, and a family to share it with. We praise you for your faithful presence on good days and not so good days. Forgive our pride and willfulness. Forgive us for sins against you and sins against those

---

1 The translation of μακάριος as blessing in Psalm 1 provides an interesting contrast. Psalm 1 explicitly refers back to the Law of Moses, which evokes both blessings and curses, suggesting that blessing is an appropriate translation. But in the context of the Sermon on the Mount, Jesus reframes social norms rather than drawing people back to the covenant and Law. Thus, social construct of honor, not the covenantal concept of blessing, is the appropriate translation.

around us. Plant in us the seeds of forgiveness and the patience to watch them grow. Plant in us the desire to follow you and to prosper your kingdom. Let us use our blessings to bless others (Gen 12:2–3)—blessing not only those easy to love but also those who need our love. Grant us strength for the day, grace for those we meet, and peace in all things. In Jesus' name, Amen.

Questions
1. Where do the Beatitudes appear in scripture?
2. What is the context for the Sermon on Mount?
3. What is the role of suffering in discipleship?
4. Where does the word, Beatitude, come from?
5. Where else in scripture do we see Beatitudes?
6. Why is the English translation, honored, to be preferred to blessed? Do you agree or disagree? Why?

PART A: TENSION WITH OURSELVES

1. HONORED ARE THE POOR IN SPIRIT

2. HONORED ARE THOSE THAT MOURN

3. HONORED ARE THE MEEK

In the first three Beatitudes, Jesus focuses on tension within ourselves and honors disciples who live humbly, mourn their fallen state, and embody a spirit of meekness. These disciples receive comfort in the journey and, at journey's end, both heaven and earth. They also experience Christian freedom journeying from the desires of the flesh to the fruits of the spirit (Gal 5:19–23).

Writing about this inward journey, Nouwen (1975) described a movement (or journey) within ourselves from loneliness to solitude.[1] This loneliness can take the form of alienation, a sense of incompleteness, or a yearning whose proper object is God, but whose current object is something other than God. Solitude differs from loneliness because it stems from communion with God and God's peace during this journey of sanctification.

---

1 The Apostle Paul speaks about journey in similar terms when he writes: *"And we all, with unveiled face, beholding the glory of the Lord, are being transformed into the same image from one degree of glory to another."* (2 Cor 3:18)

1. HONORED ARE THE POOR IN SPIRIT

1.1: Honored are the Poor in Spirit

1.2: Jesus' Mission Statement Gives Us Hope

1.3: Be Humble, Be Salt and Light

1.4: Living Out Poor in Spirit

1.1: *Honored are the Poor in Spirit*

Honored are the poor in spirit, for theirs is the kingdom of heaven. (Matt 5:3)

*J*esus chose words carefully. If he spoke Hebrew[1] rather than Greek,[2] then the First Beatitude could be stated in only 7 words[3] which aided memorization, a common first century practice because of the high cost of the written word. Because the disciples memorized his words, Jesus could speak playing word games with them, starting sentences and letting them finish them, much like a good preacher will pause to let his audience catch up.[4] Jesus also used this technique in disputing with the Pharisees, as in Matthew 21:16 where he cites the first half Psalm 8:2 and, by inference, slams them with the second half (Spangler

---

1 Bivin and Blizzard (1994, 20) argue that Jesus spoke primarily Hebrew, not Aramaic or Greek. Outside of linguistic evidence from the New Testament itself, they cite discoveries in the Dead Sea Scrolls that show commentaries written primarily in Hebrew. This suggests that the dominant language in the first century in Israel was Hebrew.

2 Common or koine Greek is the Greek found in the New Testament. Early church historian, Eusebius (Hist Eccl 3.39.16) records that Apostle Matthew wrote early drafts of his gospel for a Jewish audience in Hebrew (or Aramaic) which was later translated into Greek. More recent interpretations of Eusebius have questioned this conclusion (Knight 1992, 527).

3 Matt 5:3 HNT

4 The call and response in traditional African American preaching is famous for the dramatic pause. For example, Crawford and Troeger (1995, 17) write: *"The pause in the sermon is much more than a break in delivery that is used by skillful speakers. I see it as a metaphor of spiritual formation, as an acknowledgment by preachers that they must not cram the air so full of their words that they obscure the vast and silent mystery from which true speech arises."*

and Tverberg 2009, 38).[5] Jesus' careful choice of words and use of word associations helps us interpret the Beatitudes.

For example, the first word in the phrase in Matthew 5:3—"*Honored are the poor in spirit*"—brings to mind the first Psalm:

> *Blessed [honored] is the man who walks not in the counsel of the wicked, nor stands in the way of sinners, nor sits in the seat of scoffers; but his delight is in the law of the LORD, and on his law he meditates day and night.* (Ps 1:1–2)

The phrase, *poor in spirit*, brings to mind Isaiah 61:

> *The Spirit of the Lord GOD is upon me, because the LORD has anointed me to bring good news to the poor; he has sent me to bind up the brokenhearted, to proclaim liberty to the captives, and the opening of the prison to those who are bound; to proclaim the year of the LORD's favor, and the day of vengeance of our God; to comfort all who mourn; to grant to those who mourn in Zion—to give them a beautiful headdress instead of ashes, the oil of gladness instead of mourning, the garment of praise instead of a faint spirit; that they may be called oaks of righteousness, the planting of the LORD, that he may be glorified."* (Isa 61:1–3)

The first text, Psalm 1, plainly references the Law of Moses and the second text, Isaiah 61, references a messianic prophecy.[6] Together, by using the word—μακάριος, Jesus associates with both

---

5 Repressive cultures spawn great poetry and oral eloquence not seen in open societies, in part, because more direct speech is life-threatening.
6 The second text also appears in Jesus' own "call sermon" recorded in Luke 4.

the *Law* and *the Prophets* which for a first century Jewish audience added gravitas.

Today's commentators more normally highlight the expression, *"poor in spirit"* (οἱ πτωχοὶ τῷ πνεύματι),[7] because Luke's version of the Beatitude refers only to poor (πτωχοὶ), as in: *"honored are you who are poor, for yours is the kingdom of God."* (Luke 6:20) Poor, in this context, refers not just to low income, but to begging destitution—someone utterly dependent on God (Neyrey 1998, 170–171). As a disciple and likely eyewitness (unlike Luke[8]), Matthew's phrase, *poor in spirit*, is probably more accurate.

Taken as a whole, the First Beatitude appears hyperbolic for two reasons. The first reason is that Jesus uses a form borrowed from case law, if X, then Y. Using a legal form suggests something like the reading of a will. Second, Jesus associates things not normally associated. Unlike princes, poor do not normally inherit kingdoms; kings (those with kingdoms) are not normally humble. Thus, the First Beatitude suggests by its form and content that Jesus is using hyperbole to warm up his audience for what is obviously a serious discussion.[9]

---

7 The expression, *"poor in spirit"*, is not used elsewhere in the Bible.

8 Luke was a gentile and an associate of the Apostle Paul, not one of Jesus' disciples.

9 *"Behold my servant, whom I uphold, my chosen, in whom my soul delights; I*

The seriousness arises because the phrase, *"kingdom of heaven"*,[10] was previously associated with judgment, as in: *"Repent, for the kingdom of heaven is at hand."* (Matt 3:2, 4:17) Judgment may be implied in the converse of this Beatitude—do those who refuse to be poor in spirit (the proud) stand in opposition to the *"kingdom of heaven"*? Potentially, yes. Two candidates for judgment are almost immediately given:

> *Therefore whoever relaxes one of the least of these commandments* [in the Law and the Prophets] *and teaches others to do the same will be called least in the kingdom of heaven, but whoever does them and teaches them will be called great in the kingdom of heaven. For I tell you, unless your righteousness exceeds that of the scribes and Pharisees, you will never enter the kingdom of heaven. (Matt 5:19–20)*

Those least in the kingdom of heaven are those who teach against the law and those not to be admitted are those less righteous than the scribes and the Pharisees, according to Jesus' own words.[11]

Jesus chose words carefully.

---

have put my Spirit upon him; he will bring forth justice to the nations. He will not cry aloud or lift up his voice, or make it heard in the street; a bruised reed he will not break, and a faintly burning wick he will not quench; he will faithfully bring forth justice." (Isa 42:1–3)

10 Note that the Gospels of Mark, and Luke prefer the expression—*"kingdom of God"*—where Matthew writes—*"kingdom of heaven"* (e.g. Matt 13:31; Mark 4:30; and Luke 13:18). The Gospel of John likewise prefers to use the expression, *"kingdom of God"*, but only uses it twice in John 3.

11 *"For I tell you, unless your righteousness exceeds that of the scribes and Pharisees, you will never enter the kingdom of heaven."* (Matt 5:20)

Oh dear Lord,

I give thanks that you are ever near to me—not too proud to linger with your servant and call me friend. Bless me with your spirit of humility and generosity—generous in time, generous in friendship, and generous in sharing yourself. Keep me safe from bad company; keep me safe from pious arrogance; keep me safe from my own sinful heart. Let me always be ever near to you, now and always, through the power of your Holy Spirit. In Jesus' name, Amen.

Questions
1. What passage does the word, honored, bring to mind and why?
2. What is hyperbolic about the First Beatitude?
3. Why does the First Beatitude suggest judgment?
4. What genre (law, poetry, hyperbole, etc) do you take the Beatitudes to be?

1.2: Jesus' Mission Statement Gives Us Hope

Do not think that I have come to abolish the Law or the Prophets; I have not come to abolish them but to fulfill them. (Matt 5:17)

*I*n Matthew 5:17, Jesus offers an interpretative key that explains how to understand both his ministry on earth and his words in the Beatitudes. When Jesus said that he came to fulfill *the Law* and *the Prophets*, he means that he came to fulfill all of Old Testament scripture. In Jewish thinking, the term *"law"* brings to mind the first five books in the Old Testament—the Books of the Law (or the Pentateuch[1]): Genesis, Exodus, Leviticus, Numbers, and Deuteronomy. The term *"prophets"* loosely refers to the remainder of the Old Testament.[2] The implication is that Jesus' own words have meaning in the context of scripture because they extend it.

The Books of the Law. The Hebrew word for *poor in spirit* (לְבַשֵּׂר עֲנָוִים; *"lebaser anavim"*) also translates as: *poor, afflicted,*

1 Thoughout church history, up until the nineteenth century, no one seriously questioned that Moses wrote the Pentateuch, also called both the Book of Moses and the Book of the Law. In the nineteenth century biblical scholars began questioning Mosaic authorship because Moses' death is reported in the Deuteronomy 3:1. However, because Moses no doubt had scribes, such as Joshua, working for him, this criticism is less interesting—there is no reason to assume that all his scribes died with him. Most other reasons for questioning Mosaic authorship have subsequently been refuted.

2 In a narrower usage, the wisdom literature (Job, Psalms, Proverbs, Ecclesiastics, and Song of Solomon) and the historical books (Joshua, Judges, Ruth, 1 and 2 Samuel, 1 and 2 Kings, 1 and 2 Chronicles, Ezra, Nehemiah, and Esther) are split off from the major and minor prophets. However, prophecy and prophets are present in all of them.

humble, or meek.[3] *"Ana"*[4] appears in the Books of the Law only in Numbers 12:3 which reads: *"Now the man Moses was very meek, more than all people who were on the face of the earth."* (Num 12:3). Only Moses is described as meek and Moses' relationship with God is described as exceeding that of a typical Old Testament prophet.[5]

"Ana" invites two important observations. First, being *poor in spirit* draws us closer to God—Moses close.[6] God spoke to Moses directly, face to face, not in riddles or dreams (Num 12:6–8) which is intimacy with God rarely seen scripture since Abraham, who was described as a friend of God (Jas 2:23).

Second, if Jesus spoke Hebrew in delivering the Sermon on the Mount, then the First and the Third Beatitudes could have been expressed in the same word, *"ana"*, which would be an emphatic statement of humility. The blessing associated with *poor in spirit* was to receive *the kingdom of heaven* while the blessing for meek was to *inherit the earth*. Taken together, being *poor in spirit*

---

3 (BDB, 7237).
4 *"Ana"* is the singular for *"anavim"*.
5 *"And he said, Hear my words: If there is a prophet among you, I the LORD make myself known to him in a vision; I speak with him in a dream. Not so with my servant Moses. He is faithful in all my house. With him I speak mouth to mouth, clearly, and not in riddles, and he beholds the form of the LORD. Why then were you not afraid to speak against my servant Moses?"* (Num 12:6–8)
6 Of course, the antithesis of meek is proud, which describes Pharaoh for whom things go very badly (Exod 14:28).

(or meek) in God's eye gets you both heaven and earth, reminding us of creation (Gen 1:1) and meaning: everything.

The Books of the Prophet. The same Hebrew word for poor (עָנָו; *"ana"*) as used in Numbers 12:3[7] also appears in Isaiah 61:1–3, cited earlier. While the Books of the Prophet make many references to the poor, Isaiah 61 is quoted almost verbatim in Jesus' call sermon in Luke 4:18–19 and stands out for at least two other reasons. The first reason is that the word, *anointed*, marks this passage as a messianic prophecy. While priests, prophets, and kings were all anointed as messiahs in the Old Testament, God himself does the anointing here. The second reason is that the phrase, *"broken-hearted"* (Isa 61:1), is actually a better analogy to *"poor in spirit"* than *"poor"* and it provides another reason to prefer *"poor in spirit"* over simply *"poor"* in interpreting this Beatitude.

Fulfillment. Jesus' interpretative key is the verb, fulfill (πληρόω; *"plero"*), which generally translates as:

> to bring to a designed end, fulfill a prophecy, an obligation, a promise, a law, a request, a purpose, a desire, a hope, a duty, a fate, a destiny.[8]

In Matthew 5:17, fulfill is set in opposition to the verb, *"destroy"*,

---

7 The Greek Septuagint also uses the same word for poor as in Matt 5:3 (πτωχοῖς (Isa 61:1 BGT)).
8 (BDAG 5981, 4b).

which is usually rendered as abolish. This verbal opposition is helpful because it underscores the dynamic element in fulfill—one abolishes something static which is simply replaced with a new item. Fulfilment clearly has an expectational element (or forward drift) to it.[9] To fulfill the law is, not to replace it, but to extend it.

This idea of extending the law was new which is perhaps why Matthew felt the need to offer more explanation and uses the word, fulfill, more than the other Gospel writers.[10] In Jesus' day, for example, Rabbi's preached from the Law using the Prophets to interpret its meaning. This tradition might lead someone to say, perhaps, that the law had been *"fulfilled"* by correctly complying with it. However, the Gospel of Matthew sees prophecy fulfilled in the sense of living it out or taking the next step[11] rather than the merely honoring the boundaries of existing law.[12]

In *the Law* and *the Prophets*, we find Jesus anchored in God's creation and promises. In the word, fulfill, we find Jesus

---

9 The Greek word, τέλος—which means: *"the last part of a process, close, conclusion"* (BDAG 7310b), sums up this idea more precisely.

10 Matthew [17 times] 1:22; 2:15, 17, 23; 3:15; 4:14; 5:17; 8:17; 9:16; 12:17; 13:35, 48; 21:4; 23:32; 26:54, 56; and 27:9. Mark [5 times]1:15; 2:21; 6:43; 8:20; and 14:49. Luke [7 times] 1:20; 3:5; 4:21; 7:1; 21:24; 22:16; and 24:44. John [15 times] 1:16; 3:29; 7:8; 12:3, 38; 13:18; 15:11, 25; 16:6, 24; 17:12–13; 18:9, 32; and 19:24, 36.

11 In 12 out of 17 times.

12 Guelich (1982, 163) sees Jesus fulfilling Jeremiah 31:31–34 where God promises to write the law on our hearts.

focused on the future giving Jesus' mission both continuity and purpose.

Father God, Beloved Son, Holy Spirit,

We praise you for your example in life. In you, the Law and the Prophets are fulfilled, not in words, but in actions. We are no longer without hope—good news is preached; broken hearts are healed; and liberty is proclaimed to the captives. In you, there is jubilee; in you, there is comfort; in you, death is forever banished so that we may never mourn again. Amen and amen.

Questions
1. What is Jesus' mission statement?
2. What does the phrase, *the Law and the Prophets, mean*?
3. What is a good definition for the phrase: *poor in spirit*?
4. What is the relationship between the word, meek, and the phrase, poor in spirit and how do we know?
5. Who comes to mind in the Old Testament when you use the term meek? What about proud?
6. What is the significance of Jesus taking his call sermon (Luke 4:18–19) from Isaiah 61:1–3?
7. What does it mean to fulfill scripture?

1.3: Be Humble, Be Salt and Light

You are the salt of the earth, but if salt has lost its taste, how shall its saltiness be restored? It is no longer good for anything except to be thrown out and trampled under people's feet. (Matt 5:13)

*T*he Beatitudes introduce the Sermon on the Mount, where themes in the Beatitudes get expanded and anticipate Jesus' life and ministry. Some of these same themes are highlighted, for example, on the night of Jesus' arrest. From the Beatitudes to the sermon to the cross, Jesus' primary theme is humble witness.

Context of the Sermon. The centrality of Christian witness in Jesus' teaching is immediate and obvious, starting in the verse after the Ninth Beatitude where Jesus teaches about salt.[1] Salt is a gregarious because its usefulness comes only in combination with food—no one eats salt by itself. Salt is used to enhance the flavor of foods and to preserve them. Metaphorically, *"the disciple is to the people of the earth what salt is to food."* The disciple, who refuses to be salt, is useless and stands under judgment—*"good only to be thrown out and trampled"* (Guelich 1982, 126–127).

The centrality of witness is reinforced with a second metaphor about light (Matt 5:14–16). Clearly for Matthew the tension between the disciple and the world is real, ongoing, and at

---

1 Salt is also referenced in Mark 9:50 and Luke 14:34.

the core of the mission. At the same point Luke's account is a discussion of enemy-love (Luke 6:27–25), because without enemy-love no one can witness.

Witness is also a key to Isaiah 61:1:

> *The Spirit of the Lord GOD is upon me, because the LORD has anointed me to bring good news to the poor; he has sent me to bind up the brokenhearted, to proclaim liberty to the captives, and the opening of the prison to those who are bound . . . (Isa 61:1)*

The Messiah is anointed to *"to bring good news to the poor"* (לְבַשֵּׂר עֲנָוִים; *"lebaser anavim"*), a clear reference to witness. Notice that the Hebrew expression is only two words: the word for poor (*"anavim"*) which can mean *"poor, afflicted, humble, meek"*[2] and the word for "bring good news" (*"lebaser"*). If *humble witness* describes the Messiah and his job description, then the expression is unambiguous and applies to Jesus.[3]

Context of the Final Hours. On the night when Jesus knows that he will be arrested and his last minutes are precious, he undertakes two conspicuous acts of humility: he washes the disciples feet at the Last Super (John 13:4–5) and he prays in the Garden of Gethsemane (Matt 26:39).

2 (BDB 7238). Poor, meek and humble are captured in the same, ana, as also seen in Numbers 12:3.

3 Writing about Christian missions, Schnabel (2004, 3) observes: *"The first Christian missionary was not Paul, but Peter and Peter would not have preached a 'missionary' sermon at Pentecost if he had not been a student of Jesus for three years."*

The Gospel of John records that Jesus knew that he would soon be betrayed and die (John 13:1–3) and, while a condemned man is normally withdrawn, paralyzed with fear, and bitter, Jesus calmly begins an object-lesson about humility:

> *Jesus, knowing that the Father had given all things into his hands, and that he had come from God and was going back to God, rose from supper. He laid aside his outer garments, and taking a towel, tied it around his waist. Then he poured water into a basin and began to wash the disciples' feet and to wipe them with the towel that was wrapped around him . . . If I then, your Lord and Teacher, have washed your feet, you also ought to wash one another's feet.* (John 13:3, 4, 14)

Slaves washed most feet in the first century because most people walked barefoot (or wore only sandals) and shared the roads with work animals (who often fouled them), which made dirty, stinky feet the norm.[4] As far as we know, none of the disciples were slaves or owned slaves, but accepting a task reserved for slaves would not have been a popular object-lesson. Peter objected at first, but when he later understood the message about humility, he let Jesus wash his feet (John 13:8–9).

Foot washing is not recorded in Luke, but Luke records Jesus' teaching about humility:

> _____ *And He said to them, The kings of the Gentiles lord*

4 Walking in manure is not only dirty, it can lead to infection with parasites, such as intestinal worms.

it over them; and those who have authority over them are called Benefactors. But it is not this way with you, but the one who is the greatest among you must become like the youngest, and the leader like the servant. (Luke 22:25–26)

The importance of humility in Christian leadership and service is clear in Luke without mentioning foot washing.

While foot washing demonstrated humility before his disciples, humility before God was demonstrated in the Garden of Gethsemane where he prayed: *"My Father, if it be possible, let this cup pass from me; nevertheless, not as I will, but as you will."* (Matt 26:39) Jesus repeats this prayer three times in Matthew, underscoring the importance of this prayer (Matt 26:42–44).[5]

While Jesus' prayer in the Garden of Gethsemane displays piety, courage,[6] and humility,[7] it highlights the importance of pain and suffering in sanctification. In suffering, do we turn to God (like Jesus) or turn into our pain? When we turn to God in spite of pain, we demonstrate our faith and our identity draws more closely to Christ.[8]

---

5 Also see Mark 14:36 and Luke 22:42 which place the Garden of Gethsemane on the Mount of Olives.

6 Neyrey (1998, 110,152) sees both courage and piety.

7 The Apostle Peter and Jesus' brother, James, both echo Jesus' humility citing Proverbs 3:34: *"Toward the scorners he is scornful, but to the humble he gives favor."* (1 Peter 5:5 and James 4:6).

8 Humility is also modeled by the Apostle Paul, who writes: *"Not that I am speaking of being in need, for I have learned in whatever situation I am to be content. I know how to be brought low, and I know how to abound. In any and every circumstance, I have learned the secret of facing plenty and hunger,*

Lord of the Sabbath,

We praise you for creating us and placing us in a beautiful world, for enabling us work to support our families, and for allowing us time to rest. In this weary world, teach us to rest and to offer hospitality to those around us. In the power of your Holy Spirit, help us to be humble like salt, that flavors, preserves, and graces every table and to radiate your light when darkness threatens to overwhelm. In Jesus' precious name, Amen.

Questions
1. What is the context for the Beatitudes?
2. How many Hebrew words are required to render the phrase: *to bring good news to the poor?*
3. Why are Jesus' salt and light metaphors special?
4. What two acts of humility does Jesus perform on the night of his arrest?
5. Why is Jesus' prayer in the Garden of Gethsemane important?
6. What role does pain and suffering play in our sanctification?

---

abundance and need. I can do all things through him who strengthens me." (Phil 4:11–13) Humility is required for evangelism because of the need to interact successfully with so many strangers.

1:4: *Living Out Poor in Spirit*

So when they had come together, they asked him, Lord, will you at this time restore the kingdom to Israel? He said to them, It is not for you to know times or seasons that the Father has fixed by his own authority. But you will receive power when the Holy Spirit has come upon you, and you will be my witnesses in Jerusalem and in all Judea and Samaria, and to the end of the earth. (Acts 1:6–8)

T he First Beatitude—*Honored are the poor in spirit, for theirs is the kingdom of heaven*—pairs humility with power. Humility makes room in our lives for God but pride pushes God out.[1]

The obliqueness of the First Beatitude arises because the phrase, *kingdom of heaven,* is a round-about way of describing[2] the name of God. In Jewish tradition, the covenant name of God (YHWH) is holy and can only be properly used in the context of public worship; in other contexts, other words—such as kingdom of heaven, LORD, or, simply, the Name—are substituted out of respect for the holiness of God's name. With these substitutions, the First Beatitude might accordingly be rewritten: *honored are*

---

1 In our own sanctification, the kingdom of God breaks into our world. It is not, however, fully realized in us. It is only fully realized until Christ's return. Guelich (1982, 262) writes: *"This tension between the Kingdom present and the Kingdom future, between the fulfillment and consummation of God's promise of salvation for human history, applies not only to history but to the experience of the individual."* The kingdom of God is already here, but not yet fully realized (Ladd 1991, 57–69).

2 The technical term for *"round about way of describing"* is circumlocution.

the humble, for God will come into their life.[3]

Humility is a sign that God is welcome in our life, as the life of Abraham illustrates,[4] but the importance of humility is most clearly stated in God's response to King Solomon's prayer dedicating the first temple in Jerusalem:

> *if my people who are called by my name humble themselves, and pray and seek my face and turn from their wicked ways, then I will hear from heaven and will forgive their sin and heal their land.* (2 Chr 7:14)

Here we see that humility is a precondition for God's presence, forgiveness, and healing.

Pride, the opposite of humility, may also be an occasion for God' to enter our lives, as is revealed in Jesus' response to the disciples' impertinent question:

---

3 Understanding the First Beatitude sheds light on another distinctive teaching of Jesus. Jesus and John the Baptist both taught—*"Repent, for the kingdom of heaven is at hand."* (Matt 3:2; 4:17)—but John focused on judgment while Jesus focused on forgiveness. Because forgiveness leaves space for God's judgment and humility makes forgiveness easier, both forgiveness and humility work to make room for God in our lives (Matt 6:14–15).

4 Abraham was clearly hospitable, a kind of humility (Gen 18:2–5)), and God blesses him: *"I will bless those who bless you, and him who dishonors you I will curse, and in you all the families of the earth shall be blessed."* (Gen 12:3) God's blessing is clearly meant to be shared: Abraham is blessed to be a blessing to others. *God blesses Abraham with His presence, with sharing His plans for the future (Gen 18), and with offering His provision and protection in spite of Abraham's obvious duplicity (Gen 20). Consider also this outstanding example: "At that time Abimelech and Phicol the commander of his army said to Abraham, God is with you in all that you do. Now therefore swear to me here by God that you will not deal falsely with me or with my descendants or with my posterity"* (Gen 21:22–23).

So when they had come together, they asked him, Lord, will you at this time restore the kingdom to Israel? He said to them, It is not for you to know times or seasons that the Father has fixed by his own authority. But you will receive power when the Holy Spirit has come upon you, and you will be my witnesses in Jerusalem and in all Judea and Samaria, and to the end of the earth. (Acts 1:6–8)

In his response, Jesus tells the disciples that they cannot usurp God's sovereign authority and then, like a good supervisor, refocuses their attention on their mission.

In his explanation of their mission, Jesus refers to the two types of time, translated here as times (χρόνος; *"chronos"*) and seasons (καιρός; *"kairos"*).[5] *"Chronos"* time is time measured by a wristwatch (or calendar), which might be thought of as is a season of waiting on the Lord, while *"kairos"* time is a moment of divine revelation when the kingdom of God (the Holy Spirit) rushes in and changes everything, but according to his plans, not ours.

When we humble ourselves, we invite God to enter our lives, which can be a time of blessing, forgiveness or healing. When we do not, God acts sovereignly to accomplish his plans, with or without us.

---

5 *"Chronos"* (BDAG 7991(1), χρόνος) is translated as: *"an indefinite period of time during which some activity or event takes place, time, period of time."* *"Kairos"* (BDAD 3857(3), καιρός) is translated as: *"a period characterized by some aspect of special crisis, time."*

Humble Father, Loving Son, Ever-present Spirit,

We praise you for your mercy shown through the life, death, and

resurrection of Jesus Christ. Walk with us day by day and grant

us a humble spirit that we might enjoy your blessing, forgiveness,

and healing. Keep us focused on your mission, not our own. In

Jesus' precious name, Amen.

Questions
1. How are humility and forgiveness similar?
2. What is a circumlocution?
3. How is Jesus' use of the phrase, the kingdom of God, different from John the Baptist's?
4. How do we invited God into our lives and what are some benefits?
5. What two kinds of time are discussed in Acts 1:7–8 and how do they differ?

2. HONORED ARE THOSE THAT MOURN

2.1: Joy in Sorrow

2.2: Lament Over Sin

2.3: Death Means Resurrection

2.4: Grief Builds Character, Defines Identity

2.1: Joy in Sorrow

Honored are those who mourn, for they shall be comforted. (Matt 5:4)

T he tension within ourselves is never more obvious than when we grieve. Grief vanquishes all pretense of our self-sufficiency as we cry out to God from the bottom of our hearts and acknowledge our dependence and loss. This loss and subsequent grief is the most basic form of human suffering (France 2007, 109). Because grief and blessing sit at opposite ends of the emotional spectrum—one feels cursed, not blessed in mourning, it is paradoxical to be honored for mourning.

Mourning and comfort are brought together in Matthew's rendering of the Second Beatitude. The Greek word for mourning (πενθέω; *"pentheo"*) means—*"to experience sadness as the result of some condition or circumstance, be sad, grieve, mourn"* [1]—while the word for comfort (παρακαλέω; *"parakaleo"*) means—*"to instill someone with courage or cheer, comfort, encourage, cheer up"* [2]. Luke's rendering of the Beatitude speaks not of mourning and comfort, but of crying and laughter. [3]

---

1 (BDAG 5773 (1)).

2 (BDAG 5584(4)).

3 It is interesting that in the Second Beatitude Matthew focuses on the inward tension and release of grief (mourning/encouragement) while Luke focuses on its outward expression (crying/laughing). The Apostle Paul sees this inward tension as critically important in our spiritual formation. He writes: *"For*

In Matthew's Gospel Jesus is the object of mourning, which appears only once before and once after the Second Beatitude. Before the Beatitude, Matthew records the mourning of Jewish mothers after King Herod's slaughter of innocents in Bethlehem (Matt 2:18). Matthew cites the Prophet Jeremiah:

> *A voice is heard in Ramah, lamentation and bitter weeping. Rachel is weeping for her children; she refuses to be comforted for her children, because they are no more. (Jer 31:15)[4]*

After the Beatitude, Matthew reports Jesus telling a short parable:

> *And Jesus said to them, Can the wedding guests mourn as long as the bridegroom is with them? The days will come when the bridegroom is taken away from them, and then they will fast. (Matt 9:15)*

Because mourning accompanies both Jesus' incarnation (the slaughter of innocents) and his ascension (Jesus' parable), for Matthew the object of mourning is always Jesus.[5]

godly grief (θεὸν λύπη; "theo lupe") produces a repentance that leads to salvation without regret, whereas worldly grief produces death." (2 Cor 7:10) Paul uses an entirely different word for grief in the Greek which means: "pain of mind or spirit, grief, sorrow, affliction" (BDAG 4625). In Paul's analysis we see grief tinged with guilt and shame—a motivator for repentance.

4 Rachel died in child-birth when her second son was born. She called him— Ben-omi (son of my sorrow)—but Jacob renamed him: Benjamin (son my right hand; Gen 35:18). In the quote from Jeremiah the Greek word for weep (κλαίω) is the same word as used in Luke's Second Beatitude and it simply means: weep or cry (BDAG 4251(1)).

5 Underscoring this point, note that the stories of the widow at Nain (Luke 7:11–16) and Lazarus (John 11–12) do not appear in Matthew. A possible exception to this generalization is that hell is a place of weeping and gnashing of

If mourning requires an object, what does Jesus mourn for? Much like God mourned over sin before sending the flood (Gen 6:6), Jesus mourned over the sin of the nation of Israel, borrowing words from the Prophet Isaiah: *". . . to comfort all who mourn"* (Isa 61:2).[6] Isaiah's context, prophesy, announced the release of slaves in Babylon who previously disobeyed God and rebelled twice against the king of Babylon, Nebuchadnezzar. Because of their rebellion, Nebuchadnezzar laid siege to Jerusalem, burned the city and the temple, and took many Jewish survivors back to Babylon as slaves (2 Kgs 24 and 25).[7] In this context, Jewish salvation was literal—God would pay their ransom and redeem them from slavery, using King Cyrus of Persia to redeem them (Ezra 1:1–3).[8] Redemption of sinful slaves (rebellious Israelites) is a small step removed from redemption of slaves of sin (us).

---

teeth (ὁ κλαυθμὸς καὶ ὁ βρυγμὸς τῶν ὀδόντων; Matt 8:12, 13:42, 13:50, 22:13, 24:51, and 25:30).

6 Isaiah 61, connects the Beatitudes and Jesus' call sermon and draws attention to Jesus' role as a prophetic messiah. *"Messiah"* is the Hebrew word which corresponds to the Greek word, *"Christ"*—both mean *"anointed one"* (John 1:41; also: BDAG 4834). In Jewish tradition, prophets, kings, and priests were anointed which explains the three types of messiahs and points to three offices of Jesus' messianic ministry.

7 The experience of slavery in Babylon was on account of sin which was unlike the experience of slavery in Egypt that came about more because of a change in political fortunes (Exod 1:8).

8 In other words, salvation consisted of release from slavery, a renewed covenantal relationship with God, and restoration of the Promised Land (their inheritance)—especially Jerusalem (Jer 29:10–14).

Mourning over sin starts in Matthew with John the Baptist, *"Repent, for the kingdom of heaven is at hand"* (Matt 3:2) who draws heavily on the prophetic tradition. For example, mourning over sin starts in the Prophet Isaiah's call story:

> *And I said: Woe is me! For I am lost; for I am a man of unclean lips, and I dwell in the midst of a people of unclean lips; for my eyes have seen the King, the LORD of hosts!* (Isa 6:5)[9]

Elsewhere in the prophets we read: *"For behold, the day is coming, burning like an oven, when all the arrogant and all evildoers will be stubble."* (Mal 4:1) Facing an eternity in hell (a burning oven) for our inadequacy, brokenness, and sin (evil deeds), scripture suggests that appropriate responses include repentance, mourning, and reconciliation.[10]

Another word for mourning—woe (οὐαὶ)— is the classic expression of prophet voice and Luke uses it as a contrast immediately following μακάριος in his Beatitudes. For example, we read:

> *Honored (μακάριος) are you who are poor, for yours is the kingdom of God. . . But woe (οὐαὶ) to you who are rich, for you have received your consolation.* (Luke 6:20, 24)

---

9 Unclean lips may, for example, be an allusion to transgressing the Ninth Commandment: *"You shall not bear false witness against your neighbor."* (Exod 20:16)

10 For those of who do not believe in hell or who are thinking *"not my Jesus"*, please read: Matt 5:21–24.

In Greek, woe is an: *"interjection denoting pain or displeasure, woe, alas".*[11] Matthew uses the word, woe, eleven times, but not in the context of his Beatitudes, like Luke.[12]

Mourning is also a form of anxiety which Jesus suggests may focus on food, clothing, and the future (Matt 6:15–34).[13] Jesus goes on to conclude: *"But seek first the kingdom of God and his righteousness, and all these things will be added to you."* (Matt 6:33) Jesus' brother James completes this thought:

> *Draw near to God, and he will draw near to you . . . Be wretched and mourn and weep. Let your laughter be turned to mourning and your joy to gloom. Humble yourselves before the Lord, and he will exalt you. (Jas 4:8–10)*

Notice how James links mourning to humbling ourselves before God.[14]

---

11 (BDAG 542(1)).

12 Matt 11:21; 18:7; 23:13, 15–16, 23, 25, 27, 29; 24:19; and 26:24. The primary object of his woe, scribes and Pharisees, calls to mind the Prophet Ezekiel who writes: *"Ah, shepherds of Israel who have been feeding yourselves! Should not shepherds feed the sheep?"* (Ezek 34:2)

13 Another suggestion is anxiety about family tension or abandonment, much like Jesus himself experienced (Neyrey 1998, 172). *"Whoever loves father or mother more than me is not worthy of me, and whoever loves son or daughter more than me is not worthy of me."* (Matt 10:35–38) Also: (Matt 12:46).

14 The link in James between mourning and humbling suggests a subtle reading of the first three Beatitudes as a triad of humility—an emphatic statement. In fact, early manuscripts reverse the Second and Third Beatitudes (that is, poor in spirit, meek, mourn), suggesting textual support for this interpretation (Matt 5:4 and Matt 5:5 are reversed from common practice today. See: (Nestle-Aland 2012, 9)). Remember that *"poor in spirit"* and *"meek"* can be expressed in the same Hebrew word (עָנָו; Num 12:3). In the current ordering (that is, poor in spirit, mourn, meek) mourning is bracketed by two expres-

Jesus said: *"Honored are those who mourn, for they shall be comforted."* (Matt 5:4)

God of All Compassion,

Draw near to me in my grief, oh Lord. Let me not mourn alone, but instead turn to you. I remember how you walked with me during sunny days—days when the trees were bright with leaves and the flowers bloomed along the beach and the hills and the forest. Now that autumn has come and the days grow shorter, be ever near as a I walk along stormy paths that wind through the shadows and under leafless trees. Forgive my aloofness, ever at a distance, thinking that the sun would always shine and warm breezes would stay near. Forgive my tight-fisted attitude, grasping at time, grasping at resources, grasping for myself. Grant me a clear mind, a generous heart, and helpful hands through your Holy Spirit, Almighty God. That I might be like you—now and always. In Jesus' precious name, Amen.

---

sions for humility, which could have been done to suggest that mourning is a synonym for humility.

Questions
1. What makes the Second Beatitude paradoxical?
2. How does Matthew's treatment of this Beatitude differ from Luke's?
3. What is the primary object of mourning in Matthew?
4. What does Jesus mourn for?
5. What other words are used for mourning in the Bible?

2.2: Lament over Sin

Those who sow in tears shall reap with shouts of joy! (Ps 126:5)

*T*he Second Beatitude says those who mourn will be comforted, but what does God mourn for? In Genesis, God grieves over human wickedness:

> The LORD saw that the wickedness of man was great in the earth, and that every intention of the thoughts of his heart was only evil continually. And the LORD regretted that he had made man on the earth, and it grieved him to his heart. (Gen 6:5–6)

Human sin grieved God so much that he sent the flood, sparing only Noah, his family, and two of each animal (Gen 6:7–8).

Books of the Law. Elsewhere, studies of the word for mourning used in Matthew 5:4, associate it most often with grief over death. For example, Abraham mourns over the death of his wife, Sarah (Gen 23:2), and Joseph mourns over the death of his father, Jacob (Gen 50:3).

By contrast, studies of the word for crying used in Luke's Beatitude (Luke 6:21), associate it most often with prayer in the midst of suffering. For example, a significant point in the life of Moses arises when as a baby lying in the basket floating in the Nile he cries. On hearing Moses' crying, the daughter of Pharaoh is moved to rescue and to raise the child as her own, disobeying her father's edict to drown all Hebrew baby boys—including Moses (Exod 1:22; 2:6). Later, Moses cries to the Lord, as an act of a prayer,[1] to heal his sister, Miriam, who has be struck with leprosy and she is healed (Num 12:13).

Books of the Prophets. The focus of mourning shifts in the Books of the Prophets from death of a person to anguish—crying out—over the fate of the nation of Israel.[2]

Israel cried out to the Lord in anguish primarily because of the ups and downs of leadership in the four hundred years after leaving Egypt. Moses led the nation of Israel out of Egypt and Joshua led them into the Promised Land with strong charismatic leadership. But leadership weakened as they entered a period of the judges when, as today, *"Everyone did what was right in his own eyes."* (Judg 17:6) During the period of the judges, a cycle of sin, trouble, revival, and restoration became the normal pattern (Younger 2002, 35). The turning point in this pattern arose when the people turned and cried out (prayed) to the Lord to keep his promises:

And when all these things come upon you, the

---

1 By contrast, crying in the sense of whining or self-pity evokes God's anger (Num 11:10).

2 For example: *"My joy is gone; grief is upon me; my heart is sick within me. Behold, the cry of the daughter of my people from the length and breadth of the land: Is the LORD not in Zion? Is her King not in her? Why have they provoked me to anger with their carved images and with their foreign idols?"* (Jer 8:18–19)

> *blessing and the curse, which I have set before you,*
> *and you call them to mind among all the nations*
> *where the LORD your God has driven you, and*
> *return to the LORD your God, you and your chil-*
> *dren, and obey his voice in all that I command you*
> *today, with all your heart and with all your soul,*
> *then the LORD your God will restore your fortunes*
> *and have mercy on you, and he will gather you*
> *again from all the peoples where the LORD your*
> *God has scattered you.* (Deut 30:1–3)

In the Book of Judges this pattern of scattering, turning, deliver-

ing, and gathering repeated over and over.[3] For example,

> *But when the people of Israel cried out to the LORD,*
> *the LORD raised up a deliverer for the people of*
> *Israel, who saved them, Othniel the son of Kenaz,*
> *Caleb's younger brother. (Judg 3:9).[4]*

Later, during the period of the exile of Judah to Babylon, mourn-

ing becomes more prominent. For example, Jeremiah (the

"Mourning Prophet") wrote the Book of Lamentations; we also

read many lamentations in the Psalms. Lamentations move in

two parts, from grief to praise, for example:

> *Out of the depths I cry to you, O LORD! O Lord,*
> *hear my voice! Let your ears be attentive to the*
> *voice of my pleas for mercy! If you, O LORD,*
> *should mark iniquities, O Lord, who could stand?*
> *But with you there is forgiveness, that you may be*

---

3 Even when in the Book of Acts, the disciples are scattered, those that turned
to the Lord were gathered into churches (Acts 11:19–22).

4 A stock phrase in the Greek—ἐκέκραξαν οἱ υἱοὶ Ισραηλ—is repeated in each
case. This phrase is used at least 5 times in the Septuagint (Judg 3:9, 15; 4:3;
6:6–7; and 10:10).

feared. (Ps 130:1–4)

The heart is first emptied of bitterness; then, it opens to God.[5]

This lament form[6] also appears in the Second Beatitude, where Jesus says—*"Honored are those who mourn, for they shall be comforted."* (Matt 5:4).

This mourning over sin[7] appears as Jesus begins his journey to the cross. In the same way that God mourned over sin when preparing the great flood, Jesus he mourns over the hardness of heart of the Pharisees on the Sabbath:

> And he said to them, Is it lawful on the Sabbath to
> do good or to do harm, to save life or to kill? But
> they were silent. And he looked around at them with
> anger, grieved at their hardness of heart, and said
> to the man, Stretch out your hand. He stretched it
> out, and his hand was restored. The Pharisees went
> out and immediately held counsel with the Herodi-
> ans against him, how to destroy him. (Mark 3:4–6)

Here when Mark writes about the hardness of heart, he is comparing the Pharisees to Pharaoh (Exod 4:21).

The narrative in Mark 3 is also significant because it

---

5 The division in Psalm 130 between mourning and praise occurs in verse four with the word, but: *"But with you there is forgiveness.."* (Ps 130:4)

6 Christian songwriter Michael Card (2005, 19) writes at length about lament. A lament has two parts. The first part is cathartic—we pour out our hearts to God emptying ourselves of the anger, fear, hatred, and other vile emotions that we harbor. Once this catharsis is complete, then in part two are hearts are open to remember God grace and mercy to us in the past and we are able to praise God from the bottom of our hearts.

7 What the Apostle Paul calls: *"godly grief"* (2 Cor 7:10).

explicitly links human suffering to sin and God's grief. Mark 3 *"is the only passage in the gospels where Jesus is said to be angry.* (Elliott 2006, 214). Jesus gets angry, because *"The Sabbath was made for man, not man for the Sabbath."* (Mark 2:27) and Jesus cares about the well-being of people more than he cares about Sabbath observance (or the Pharisee's conception of the political restoration of the nation of Israel).[8] Because Jesus cares about suffering people, we should too.

Compassionate Father,

Be especially near me this morning—blot out my guilt; hide my shame; cover up my sin. Though I am unworthy, share an intimate moment with me. Remind me of better times. Grant me a new day in the sunshine of your mercy—a day when I could lose myself in your love and extend your love with abandon to those around me. Open a bridge over the gaps that separate us—time and holiness and power—that I might spend more time with

---

8 This chain of reasoning—belief, contrary action, emotional response—is an example of the cognitive theory of emotions where emotions flow out of our judgment or thinking rather than arising spontaneously in some unexplained manner (Elliott 2006, 31). Lester (2007, 14–16,106) agrees. He sees anger as a response to a threat to basic values and beliefs what can help us sort out our true feelings.

those around me, might share in your holy affections, might overcome my own weaknesses and bitterness, and turn to you, instead of into my pain, that I may experience godly, redemptive grief. Through the power of your Holy Spirit and in Jesus' name, Amen.

Questions
1. What do you mourn for? What does God mourn for?
2. How does mourning differ in the Old Testament between the Books of the Law and the Books of the Prophets?
3. What are the objects of mourning and crying in the Old Testament?
4. What is Godly grief?
5. What are the two parts of a lament and why do we care?
6. Where do we see the lament form in the New Testament?
7. What is special about Mark 3:4–6?

2.3: Death Means Resurrection

When Jesus saw her weeping, and the Jews who had come with her also weeping, he was deeply moved in his spirit and greatly troubled. And he said, Where have you laid him? ... When he had said these things, he cried out with a loud voice, Lazarus, come out. (John 11:33–43)

The two-part form of a lament sets us on a spiritual journey—when Jesus weeps, the dead are raised;[1] when Jesus dies, our lives are redeemed and we find hope (1 Pet 1:3), as outlined by the Apostle Paul:

> *that I may know him and the power of his resurrection, and may share his sufferings, becoming like him in his death, that by any means possible I may attain the resurrection from the dead. (Phil 3:10–11)*

Paul advises us to imitate Christ and to place our emotions in God's service[2] so that the world might too be redeemed.[3]

Mourning is redeemed in Christian hope. The hope of resurrection permits us to look beyond the grief in this life to our future in Christ, as the Prophet Jeremiah wrote so eloquently:

> *For I know the plans I have for you, declares the LORD, plans for welfare and not for evil, to give you a future and a hope. (Jer 29:11)*

---

1 Also: Mark 5:38–41; Luke 5:13–15.

2 *"Bless those who persecute you; bless and do not curse them. Rejoice with those who rejoice, weep with those who weep."* (Rom 12:14–15)

3 Jer 4:28; Rom 8:22.

We hear an echo of Jeremiah in the Sermon on the Mount, when he writes about anxiety:

> *Therefore I tell you, do not be anxious about your life, what you will eat or what you will drink, nor about your body, what you will put on. Is not life more than food, and the body more than clothing?* (Matt 6:25)

Anxiety is a form of grieving over life's daily challenges—what to eat or what to wear—in a kind of despair over present circumstances.

As Christians, we know that present circumstances give way to a future in Christ—death does not have the final word (1 Thess 4:13). Because our future is in Christ, we are like children who can delight in hearing scary stories knowing that the stories have a happy ending.

The Apostle Paul writes: *"For godly grief [θεὸν λύπη; "theo lupe"] produces a repentance that leads to salvation without regret, whereas worldly grief produces death."* (2 Cor 7:10) The word for grief that Paul uses means: *"pain of mind or spirit, grief, sorrow, affliction"*.[4] We grieve over our sin; we lament over our brokenness; and once we have poured it all out, we turn to God and repent, as the Psalmist writes:

> *Those who sow in tears shall reap with shouts of*

---

4 (BDAG 4625).

joy! He who goes out weeping, bearing the seed for sowing, shall come home with shouts of joy, bringing his sheaves with him. (Ps 126:5–6)

This sounds similar to Luke's version of the Second Beatitude:

"Honored are you who weep now, for you shall laugh." (Luke 6:21)

Through godly grief and repentance God gently leads us to salvation.

Lamb of God,

Thank you for the hope that comes in the midst of life and death. Be especially present with those that grieve—grieve over the loss of a loved one, grieve over a life not lived according to plan, grieve over sin and brokenness and shame. Show us the road to recovery, wholeness, and restoration; show us the plans that you have laid out for us—plans for welfare, not evil, for a future, and a hope in you. Grant us godly grief that produces repentance and redemption and new life in joy. In the power of your Holy Spirit, wipe away our tears so that we might behold the Father. In Jesus' name, Amen.

Questions

1. What is godly grief? How does it differ from other grief?
2. What steps in imitating Christ does Paul see? What is the nature of Christian hope?
3. How is anxiety like grief? How do they differ?
4. Why is there tension between hope and grief?

2.4: Grief Builds Character, Defines Identity

Then *he said to them, My soul is very sorrowful, even to death; remain here, and watch with me. And going a little farther he fell on his face and prayed, saying, My Father, if it be possible, let this cup pass from me; nevertheless, not as I will, but as you will.* (Matt 26:38–39)

*T*he emotional tension within ourselves is never greater than when we mourn, which requires a decision: do we turn into our pain in self-pity or do we turn to God in faith? Standing in the shadow of the cross at Gethsemane, Jesus turned to God when he faced this decision.

The decisions we make and the pains we bear shape our identity because they are both unavoidable and costly—we do not normally choose to experience pain.[1] Pain and grief transform us and that is why the only emotion that appears in the Beatitudes is grief.

We grieve when we lose something important to us. In writing about the second Beatitude, Evangelist Billy Graham (1955, 20–26) identified five objects of mourning:

1. Inadequacy—before you can grow strong, you must recognize your own weakness

2. Repentance—before you can ask for forgive-

---

1 *"Through the CALL of Jesus men become individuals. Whilly-nilly, they are compelled to decide, and that decision can only be made by themselves."* (Bonhoeffer 1995, 94)

ness, you must recognize your sin;

3. Love—our compassion for suffering of brothers and sisters takes the form of mourning and measures our response to Christ's commandment to love God and love our neighbor,[2]

4. Soul travail—groaning for the salvation of the lost; and

5. Bereavement—mourning over those that have passed away.

These objects of grief can also be categorized functionally, as:

1. Material loss;

2. Relationship loss;

3. Intra-psychic loss—loss of a dream;

4. Functional loss—including loss of autonomy;

5. Role loss—like retirement; and

6. Systemic loss—like departure from your family of origin (Mitchell and Anderson 1983, 36–45).

Each loss is unique and must be separately grieved which takes time and energy. When we neglect to take the time to grieve our losses, the grief does not make magically disappear; it can come back in the form of sudden outbreaks of anxiety or depression without obvious explanation—emotional hijackings. We try to

---

2 Matt 22:36–40.

avoid grief because it reminds us of our mortality and, in doing so, frequently challenges the flawed assumptions that we prefer to live by.

Loss and grief were not always ignored, as my grandfather taught me when my grandmother suffered from Alzheimer's disease. In spite of being over one hundred years old, my grandfather expressed his love by caring for her at home and set an example of sacrificial love and faithfulness that I will never forget.

Saint Francis of Assisi said it best:

> Lord, grant that I may seek rather
>
> To comfort than to be comforted,
>
> To understand than to be understood,
>
> To love than to be loved;
>
> For it is by giving that one receives,
>
> It is by self-forgetting that one finds,
>
> It is by forgiving that one is forgiven,
>
> It is by dying that one awakens to eternal life.3

The griefs we bear and the choices we make strengthen our faith, define our character, and temper our relationships, working in us like the refiner's fire (Mal 3:3).

Jesus teaches: *"Honored are those who mourn, for they*

3 (Graham 1955, 24).

shall be comforted." (Matt 5:4)

Almighty Father,

I praise you for your enduring presence and manifest glory all around. Your glory wakes me in the morning; its sustains my days; and it protects me during the night. Empty me of all despair and bitterness that deflate my life. Help me to confess my weaknesses, my brokenness, and my sin to make room for your glory, your mercy, and your love. Heal me with your presence when only your presence will do. Bind up my wounds; give me hope; and guide me in your ways that I might see the new day that you have prepared for me. In the power of your Holy Spirit and in Jesus' precious name, Amen.

Questions
1. What is a Gethsemane moment?
2. What decision does grief pose for us and how does this decision form our character?
3. What is the only emotion cited in the Beatitudes and why?
4. What are the five objects of mourning cited by Billy Graham? What are six types of losses?

5. Why is it important to grieve our losses? What is emotional hijacking?

6. What do you remember most about your grandparents or other loved ones that have passed?

3. HONORED ARE THE MEEK

3.1: Resolve Tension into Identity

3.2: Meekness Speaks Volumes

3.3: Meek is the Pastoral Gene

3.4: Lead Out of Meekness

3.1: Resolve Tension into Identity

But the meek shall inherit the land and delight themselves in abundant peace. (Ps 37:11)

O ne resolution of life's tensions is that they are absorbed into our identity, defining our self-image, relationships, and expected actions and reactions. A pastoral identity, for example, implies spending time with God, interpreting scripture, praying with others, preaching the Gospel, and offering comfort to everyone; these activities are expected of pastors and are an essential part of pastoral training. Likewise, training in humility makes us meek, part of our identity as disciples of Christ.

The Third Beatitude is unique to Matthew: *"Honored are the meek, for they shall inherit the earth."* (Matt 5:5). Meek means to: *"...not [be] overly impressed by a sense of one's self-importance, gentle, humble, considerate".*[1] Meek is like applied humility (poor in spirit)—a character trait of being humble,[2] suggested by at least three verses in Matthew:

> *1. Take my yoke upon you, and learn from me, for I am gentle and lowly in heart, and you will find rest for your souls. (Matt 11:29)*

> *2. Say to the daughter of Zion, 'Behold, your king is coming to you, humble, and mounted on a donkey,*

1 (BDAG 6132).

2 *"...there is little or no difference between the poor and the meek in the Psalms or Isaiah..."* (Guelich 1982, 82)

on a colt, the foal of a beast of burden. (Matt 21:5)

3. And the high priest stood up and said, Have you no answer to make? What is it that these men testify against you? But Jesus remained silent. (Matt 26:62–63)

In these three events—Jesus' invitation to discipleship, his humble parade into Jerusalem, and his silence while on trial—Jesus exhibited his meekness.[3] Jesus' meekness is also observed in the writings of the Apostles Peter, James, and Paul.[4]

In his writing, Neyrey (1998, 181–182) describes honor in meekness in these terms:

> *...It can indeed be understood as grounds for praise for refusing to be a victim...according to the choreography of honor challenges, the 'meek' person could be one who makes no honor claims (e.g. Matt 21:5), or, more likely, one who does not give a riposte [response] to challenges and does not respond in anger to insults. In this light, a 'meek' person disengages entirely from the typical honor games of the village...failure to seek revenge.*

The implication here is that the meek person choses wisely to remain silent, especially when speaking would escalate conflict with another person.

The problem of escalation is referenced in the Sermon on the Mount when Jesus said:

---

3 Sedler (2003, 92) observes that *"anything Jesus said would have been twisted, turned, and rejected."*

4 See for example: 1 Pet 3:13–17, Jas 1:21, and 2 Cor 10:1.

1. ...everyone who is angry with his brother will be liable to judgment; whoever insults his brother will be liable to the council; and whoever says, You fool! will be liable to the hell of fire. (Matt 5:22)

2. Let what you say be simply Yes or No; anything more than this comes from evil. (Matt 5:37)[5]

3. Do not resist the one who is evil.[6] But if any-one slaps you on the right cheek, turn to him the other also. And if anyone would sue you and take your tunic, let him have your cloak as well. And if anyone forces you to go one mile, go with him two miles. (Matt 5:39–41)

In other words, the meek person will refuse to pursue vindication, offer no response when baited to act imprudently, or just make peace. We are to preserve a humble identity by refusing to argue, belittle, or engage in a response to harsh words. In other words, defend your meekness with silence and humility.

Ortberg (2012, 107) illustrates Jesus' meekness in imaging a pep talk that Jesus might have given the disciples:

Here's our strategy. We have no money, no clout, no status, no buildings, no soldiers... We will tell them[7] all that they are on the wrong track... When they

---

5 The context for these words was admonishment to resist the temptation to use an oath.

6 Savage (1996, 57–61) offers an interesting application of this principle of not resisting evil which he refers to as *"fogging"*. When one is criticized, one responds by finding something in the criticism to agree with—even if only implied. This frustrates the attacker and keeps one from becoming defensive. Jesus employs a variation on this approach when asked about taxes (Matt 22:17–22).

7 Jewish and Romans leaders, Zealots, collaborators, Essenes.

hate us—and a lot of them will...we won't fight back, we won't run away, and we won't give in. We will just keep loving them...That's my strategy.

Meekness is a strategy, not a weakness, that identifies us Christians, advances the kingdom, and steals the thunder from our adversaries.

Humble Lord,

Help us to rest in you—to bear the burdens that you bore, to exhibit the grace that you exhibited, and to extend the peace that you extended. Clear our cluttered minds and still our restless hearts so that we refuse to point the finger, refuse to be victims, and resolve to roll up our sleeves to help those around us and love our enemies. Heal us of our anxieties and restore us to the person that you created us be. Through the power of your Holy Spirit and in Jesus' precious name, Amen.

Questions
1. How are life's tensions sometimes resolved?
2. What does it mean to place our identity in Christ and not in

circumstances?

3. How do you define meekness? Was Jesus meek?

4. What is an honor game? How do the meek respond?

5. What does John Ortberg say about Jesus' strategy in evangelism and why is it interesting?

6. How does meekness differ from weakness?

3.2: Meekness Speaks Volumes

Now the man Moses was very meek, more than all people who were on the face of the earth. (Num 12:3)

*B*ecause meekness is not a natural state, but a fruit of the Spirit, we must learn to be meek.[1] If Jesus is meek, does that imply that God learned to be meek? What does the Old Testament suggest about God's meekness?

The Books of the Law. Moses is described as meek and, because he has an especially intimate relationship with God (Num 12:3), Moses' meekness infers that God may also be meek,[2] as inferred in narratives about God as creator, covenant maker, and destroyer by means of the flood of that floated Noah's ark.

As creator, God is pictured as sovereign issuing decrees, such as: *"And God said, Let there be light, and there was light."* (Gen 1:3) How light came to be, we are not told; we are only told that God decreed that it be done—God is verbal, but he is not chatty. God's next statement is a declaration: *"And God saw that*

1 *Now the works of the flesh are evident: sexual immorality, impurity, sensuality, idolatry, sorcery, enmity, strife, jealousy, fits of anger, rivalries, dissensions, divisions, envy, drunkenness, orgies, and things like these. I warn you, as I warned you before, that those who do such things will not inherit the kingdom of God. But the fruit of the Spirit is love, joy, peace, patience, kindness, goodness, faithfulness, gentleness, self-control; against such things there is no law. (Gal 5:19–23)*

2 We are all created in God's image which suggests that Moses' meekness is, in fact, part of that image. Alternatively, we could just say that: *birds of a feather flock together*—the bonds of friends are most easily formed with people just like us.

the light was good." (Gen 1:4)—God does not brag; he meekly observes. While his ability to create illustrates God's power, God is—*"...not overly impressed by a sense of [one's] self-importance, gentle, humble, considerate".*[3] In other words, creating is *"no big deal"* for our meek God.

As covenant maker, God is objective and thoughtful, not vengeful and domineering. The covenant with Adam, for example, is mostly implicit because God creates Adam and Eve, gives them a mandate (be fruitful and multiply), sets them in a garden, and leaves only one limitation—do not eat from the tree of the knowledge of good and evil. When Adam and Eve disobey God's limitation, he does not replace them with another couple; instead, God punishes (curses) them and sends them out of the garden. But before they go, like a mother preparing her child for the first day of school, *"God made for Adam and for his wife garments of skins and clothed them."* (Gen 3:21) While God was perfectly in his right as covenant maker to be harsh with Adam and Eve, in fact, he treated them gently—another indication of meekness.

As destroyer, God sends a flood to wipe out humanity and every living thing—almost. The writer of Genesis records God's motivation as follows:

3 (BDAG 6132).

> *The LORD saw that the wickedness of man was great in the earth, and that every intention of the thoughts of his heart was only evil continually. And the LORD regretted that he had made man on the earth, and it grieved him to his heart. So the LORD said, I will blot out man whom I have created from the face of the land, man and animals and creeping things and birds of the heavens, for I am sorry that I have made them. But Noah found favor in the eyes of the LORD. (Gen 6:5–8)*

The key words here are: *regretted that he had made man on the earth, and it grieved him to his heart;* God is moved by regret and by grief over sin—not anger—to send the flood, which is not the image of a wrathful God that some advance.

In spite of the flood, God is careful to spare Noah, his family, and a pair of each of the animals. The ark with Noah, his family, and the animals is a prototype of the remnant of Israel later spared during the Babylonian exile.[4] Choosing to exercise only a subset of his rights with the remnant—like a parent offering discipline, not a judge imposing legal penalties—is another example of a meek God.

These examples of God as creator, as covenant maker, and as destroyer give us a picture of a God who does not need to learn to be meek, because he was already meek when he created

---

4 The Prophet Isaiah introduces this motif with these words: *"This is like the days of Noah to me: as I swore that the waters of Noah should no more go over the earth, so I have sworn that I will not be angry with you, and will not rebuke you."* (Isa 54:9)

the heavens and the earth.

The Books of the Prophets. The words, meek and humble, appear throughout the Books of the Prophets where Guelich (1982, 82) observed that: *"there is little or no difference between the poor and the meek in the Psalms or Isaiah".* This observation makes perfect sense because the nation of Israel spent much of that period as slaves exiled in Babylon and meekness is referred to often, as in:[5]

> *1. There shall come forth a shoot from the stump of Jesse, and a branch from his roots shall bear fruit. And the Spirit of the LORD shall rest upon him, the Spirit of wisdom and understanding, the Spirit of counsel and might, the Spirit of knowledge and the fear of the LORD... but with righteousness he shall judge the poor, and decide with equity for the meek of the earth; and he shall strike the earth with the rod of his mouth, and with the breath of his lips he shall kill the wicked. Righteousness shall be the belt of his waist, and faithfulness the belt of his loins. (Isa 11:1–5)*

> *2. He leads the humble in what is right, and teaches the humble his way. (Ps 25:9)*

> *3. But the meek shall inherit the land and delight themselves in abundant peace. (Ps 37:11)*

> *4. Rejoice greatly, O daughter of Zion! Shout aloud, O daughter of Jerusalem! Behold, your king is coming to you; righteous and having salvation is he,*

---

5 Missing from this list is Isaiah 61:1, which has already been mentioned multiple times.

> humble and mounted on a donkey, on a colt, the
> foal of a donkey. (Zec 9:9)

The appearance of meekness in these messianic passages suggests that the prophets considered meekness a divine attribute.

Fulfillment. The meekness that appears in the Old Testament is both a character attribute of God—part of his transcendence—and a kind of solidarity between God and his people. Elliot (2006, 123) notes that *"Israel's God was emotionally stable";* God meekness typifies this stability, which has led theologians to coin the term, immutability,[6] meaning that God's character does not change.[7] Thus, when Jesus describes himself as gentle or meek (Matt 11:29), a Jewish audience might rightly hear such words as a messianic claim.[8]

---

6 Consider the converse—what if God's character evolved and was not immutable? What if God changed his mind and did not tell us? In such a changing world, the promises of the Bible could also change at any time—which part of the Bible is still true? What if the atonement of Christ was no longer sufficient?

7 *"For I the LORD do not change; therefore you, O children of Jacob, are not consumed."* (Mal 3:6) Horton (2011, 235) writes: *"Building on a patristic consensus, Thomas Aquinas argued that God is actus purus ('pure act'), which means that there are no potentialities in God. Complete and perfect in himself from eternity to eternity, God has no potential that is not already fully realized. God cannot be more infinite, loving, or holy tomorrow than today. If God alone is necessary and independent of all external conditions, fully realized in all of his perfections, then there is literally nothing for God to become."*

8 God's meekness is just one aspect of His immutable character. Truth is another (Exod 34:6). God's immutable character implies that only one, objective truth exists. Jesus said: *"I am the way, and the truth, and the life. No one comes to the Father except through me."* (John 14:6) The implication is that God's immutable character anchors stability in the physical and spiritual realms providing credibility also to the authority of scripture.

We hear meekness as typifying God's immutable character which provides a foundation for our faith. For us, meekness is a fruit of the spirit, but, for God, it is just who he is.

Amazing Lord,

Creator of all that is, that was, and that will ever be. You are glorious and loving; humble and holy. Teach me to be like you—to love your laws like Moses; to love your grace like Christ; to trust in your compassion, meekness, and strength. Use me to build on the work of Christ—to comfort the afflicted, to aid the poor, to offer gentleness and hospitality, and to suffer for his name's sake. Grant me the strength to learn and the desire to apply my lessons. Give me eyes that see, ears that hear, and hands that are open. In the power of your Holy Spirit and in Jesus' name, Amen.

Questions
1. What is learning? Does God learn?
2. Do the Books of the Law suggest that God is meek? How do we know?
3. Is God emotionally stable? What evidence do we have?

4. What emotion does God exhibit in Genesis 6? Was it expected?
5. What is the nature of God's wrath?
6. What is the difference between poor and meek in the Books of the Prophets?
7. What is immutability?

3.3: Meek is the Pastoral Gene

Take my yoke upon you, and learn from me, for I am gentle and lowly in heart, and you will find rest for your souls. (Matt 11:29)

*M*eekness is a pastoral characteristic[1] which we know not only from the words of Jesus, but also from his disciples and those that followed. For example, Jesus says:

> *And whoever gives one of these little ones even a cup of cold water because he is a disciple, truly, I say to you, he will by no means lose his reward.* (Matt 10:42)

Here he is encouraging his disciples to display humility lived out (or meekness) in front of, not children (*"little ones"*), but young believers (or seekers).[2] The word for disciple (μαθητής; *"mathetes"*) here means—*"one who engages in learning through instruction from another, pupil, apprentice"*[3]—and Jesus' disciples were instructed to teach young believers with an attitude of gentleness and service, modeling meekness in what they said and did.

The Apostle Paul paraphrases Jesus' command, making teaching meekness (or gentleness) an explicit requirement for church leaders, as when he writes:

> *And the Lord's servant must not be quarrelsome but kind to everyone, able to teach, patiently en-*

---

1 Colson (2005, 30) writes: *"Freedom lies in obedience to our calling."*
2 Matt 10:42; 18:6, 10, 14, Mark 9:42, Luke 17:2.
3 (BDAG, 4662).

*during evil, correcting his opponents with gen-
tleness. God may perhaps grant them repentance
leading to a knowledge of the truth, and they may
come to their senses and escape from the snare of
the devil, after being captured by him to do his will.*
(2 Tim 2:24–26)

Gentleness (or meekness) also appears on many of Paul's lists of

the fruits of the spirit[4] and in the writing of James and Peter.[5]

Interestingly, meekness is cloaked in one of the most fa-

mous images of Christ: *"I am the good shepherd. The good shep-*

herd lays down his life for the sheep." (John 10:11) The image of

the Good Shepherd is, in fact, a messianic image prophesied by

Isaiah in one of his Servant Song passages:

*He will tend his flock like a shepherd; he will gath-
er the lambs in his arms; he will carry them in his
bosom, and gently lead those that are with young.*
(Isa 40:11)

The Apostle John pushes the shepherd metaphor even further

when he writes:

*For the Lamb in the midst of the throne will be
their shepherd, and he will guide them to springs
of living water, and God will wipe away every tear
from their eyes.* (Rev 7:17)

---

4 (e.g. Gal 5:19–23; Col 3:12–14).

5 James, Jesus' half-brother, and leader of the church in Jerusalem likewise
writes: *"Who is wise and understanding among you? By his good conduct let
him show his works in the meekness of wisdom."* (Jas 3:13) The Apostle Peter
admonishes us to practice apologetics also with meekness: *"always being prepared to make a defense to anyone who asks you for a reason for the hope that
is in you; yet do it with gentleness and respect"* (1 Pet 3:15)

Here the messianic shepherd is also both a lamb and a king, underscoring that meekness is a divine attribute.

Shepherding likewise anchors the great pastoral passage in the Gospel of John where the risen Christ confronts and restores Peter to leadership:

> *Simon, son of John, do you love me more than these? He said to him, Yes, Lord; you know that I love you. He said to him, Feed my lambs.* (John 21:15)

Three times Jesus asks if Peter loves him and with each of Peter's responses he asks Peter to give up fishing (catching fish with hooks and nets) and to take up shepherding (caring for, defending, and feeding sheep; John 21:15–18). As with Peter, Jesus bids all his disciples to care for his flock displaying meekness.

Beloved Good Shepherd,

We praise you for your teaching heart and gentle spirit. We thank you for modeling meekness in leadership and for your patience with us as we learn. Heal our hearts, humble our spirits, open our hands that we might lead with gentleness and hospitality. Grant us open minds and a teachable spirit that we might lead those around us only to you. Through the power of your Holy Spirit,

now and always, Amen.

Questions
1. Are pastor's normally and naturally meek? Why or why not?
2. What does Matthew mean by the term: *"little ones"*?
3. What characteristics does the Apostle Paul seek in church leaders?
4. What do Peter and James say about meekness?
5. Why is a shepherd meek?

3.4: Lead Out of Meekness

For *the Lamb in the midst of the throne will be their shepherd, and he will guide them to springs of living water, and God will wipe away every tear from their eyes.* (Rev 7:17)

*M*eekness marks a natural leader, yet few aspire to be meek,[1] as Nouwen (1989, 82) observes:

> Christian leadership...is not leadership of power and control, but a leadership of powerlessness and humility in which the suffering servant of God, Jesus Christ, is made manifest.[2]

Like the one who sent him,[3] the ideal Christian leader is meek, but meekness also creates tension within us it, between us, and with God, to which we will now turn.

Tension Within. For church leaders, the Apostle Paul advises elders and deacons to pursue fruits of the spirit, such as *"righteousness, godliness, faith, love, steadfastness, gentleness"* (1

---

1 *"No grace is less prayed for, or less cultivated than gentleness."* (Bridges 1996, 180)

2 Nouwen (1989, 7–8) sees these tests as common leadership temptations— the temptation to be relevant, be powerful, and be spectacular. Scazzero (2006, 75–78) phrases these temptations more personally as the temptation to perform, to possess, and to be popular.

3 After his baptism, Jesus: *"was led by the Spirit in the wilderness for forty days, being tempted by the devil."* (Luke 4:1–2) The devil posed three tests: turn a stone into bread; become my vassal; and throw yourself down (Luke 4:4, 7, 9). Jesus responds to these tests by calmly citing three passages from the Book of Deuteronomy: *"...man lives by every word that comes from the mouth of the LORD."* (Deut 8:3) *"It is the LORD your God you shall fear. Him you shall serve and by his name you shall swear."* (Deut 6:13) *"You shall not put the LORD your God to the test..."* (Deut 6:16)

Tim 6:11), where gentle is a good synonym for meek. In pursuing fruits like meekness, however, success is not easy to obtain. Even Paul points to inner tension:

> For I have the desire to do what is right, but not the ability to carry it out. For I do not do the good I want, but the evil I do not want is what I keep on doing. (Rom 7:18–19)

As with any fruit of the spirit, progress in obtaining meekness requires the intervention of the Holy Spirit.

Tension With Others. "*Isn't meekness a personal attribute?*" A friend recently inquired. "*How can you be meek when you are responsible for other people?*" One response is that modeling meekness creates space in our lives for other people, which is foundational for servant leadership.

During his time in prison, for example, Bonhoeffer continued to function sacrificially as a pastor offering counsel to other inmates and even the prison guards. When offered an opportunity to escape from prison, Bonhoeffer refused to leave because escaping would put his family outside prison and his ministry inside prison at risk (Metaxas 2010, 448).

Sacrificial leadership can be risky, painful, and, yet, unappreciated, as the Apostle Paul writes:

> But we have this treasure in jars of clay, to show that the surpassing power belongs to God and not

to us. We are afflicted in every way, but not crushed; perplexed, but not driven to despair; persecuted, but not forsaken; struck down, but not destroyed; always carrying in the body the death of Jesus, so that the life of Jesus may also be manifested in our bodies. (2 Cor 4:7–10)

Several levels of meekness may need to be developed.

Tension With God. Sacrificial leadership can also lead to the cross. In a moment of weakness and despair on the cross Jesus cried: *"My God, my God, why have you forsaken me?"* (Mark 15:34), words taken from Psalm 22:1 that later ends in praise: *"You who fear the LORD, praise him!"* (Ps 22:23) Emptied of our despair, we are able again to turn to God in praise.

We can lead with meekness, even in the face of suffering, in part, because the story does not end in suffering. Just like the cross of Christ is followed by the resurrection of Christ; when we share in his suffering we know that we will also share in his victory.[4] As the Apostle Paul writes: *"O death, where is your victory? O death, where is your sting?"* (1 Cor 15:55) Because our future is in Christ, today we can embrace Christ's meekness.

---

4 *"For as we share abundantly in Christ's sufferings, so through Christ we share abundantly in comfort too."* (2 Cor. 1:5)

Almighty Father,

We give thanks for the gift of faith and the call into ministry which reaches out to our families, friends, and beyond. Guard our hearts in times of weakness, hardship, and temptation. Keep our mind sharp so that we offer you our praise with clarity, coherence, and dedication, not tainted by vain desires, cultural confusion, or subtle idolatries. Grant us a spirit of meekness, a spirit of humility seated deeply in our character—not loosely held, superficially worn, or overshadowed by cherished sins. Place in us hearts eager to pursue righteousness, godliness, faith, love, steadfastness, and gentleness. Give us the assurance of your providence so we can offer sacrificial hospitality to those around us. In the face of suffering, make your Holy Spirit especially visible so that we would not fail in our ministry due to temptations to be relevant, powerful, or spectacular in the eyes of those in our care. In the strong name of Jesus Christ, your Son and our Savior. Amen.

Questions

1. Why is meekness a trait of natural leaders?
2. How does sacrificial leadership contribute to tension within ourselves, with others, and with God?
3. Does the Apostle Paul attain sanctification? How do sacrificial leadership and meekness relate?
4. What are Jesus' three temptations? How does Henri Nouwen interpret them?

PART B: TENSION WITH GOD

4. HONORED ARE THOSE THAT HUNGER AND THIRST

5. HONORED ARE THE MERCIFUL

6. HONORED ARE THE PURE IN HEART

In Beatitudes four, five, and six, we move from tension with ourselves to tension with God. Jesus speaks of God's righteousness, mercy, and purity; aspects of God's holiness unattainable in the flesh. Sinful compared with God's holiness and finite compared with God infinite nature, we experience tension with God. Yet, created in the image of God (Gen 1:28) and redeemed by His Son, Jesus Christ, we hunger for God's righteousness (Phil 3:8–9)—a precious thing in a fallen world.

Writing about what he calls *"the upward journey"*, Nouwen (1975) describes us as moving from illusion to prayer. Like the man lost and dying of thirst in the desert chases after an illusion of water, our idolatrous selves chase after illusions of divinity offered by the idols of this world. The Holy Spirit sets us free from these illusions and allows us to approach God through Jesus Christ, who invites us to give up our illusions and enter into relationship with God in prayer.

Jesus honors those who are passionate about their relationship with God, who offer his mercy to others, and who seek to be holy, in the next three Beatitudes.

4. HONORED ARE THOSE THAT HUNGER AND THIRST

4.1: Jesus: Passionately Seek the Kingdom of God

4.2: Hunger and Thirst for God

4.3: Fools for Christ

4.4: In Jesus Completeness is Restored

4.1: Jesus: Passionately Seek the Kingdom of God

Honored are those who hunger and thirst for righteousness, for they shall be satisfied. (Matt 5:6)

*T*he Fourth Beatitude taps into deep physical and spiritual needs expressed in the words: *"hunger and thirst for righteousness"*. Hunger (πεινάω; *"penao"*) means both *"to feel the pangs of lack of food, hunger, be hungry"* and to *"desire something—strongly, hunger for something"*[1] while thirst (διψάω; *"lepsao"*) means both *"to have a desire for liquid, be thirsty, suffer from thirst"* and *"to have a strong desire to attain some goal, thirst, i.e. long for something"*.[2] Righteousness (δικαιοσύνη; *"dikaosune"*) means the *"quality or state of juridical correctness with focus on redemptive action, righteousness"*,[3] which we hunger and thirst for in a sinful world.

The theme of hungering and thirsting—deep need and abundant provision—runs throughout in John's Gospel. Jesus first reveals himself to a couple of newlyweds in danger of being stigmatized for their poverty, lacking sufficient wine to meet community hospitality standards. Our insufficiencies are contrasted with God's super-abundant provision—of wine (John

---

1 (BDAG 5758). (Matt 5:6; Luke 6:21).
2 (BDAG 2051).
3 (BDAG 2004(2)).

2:1–11), bread (John 6:5–14), and fish (John 21:3–13)—which displays God's trademark generosity.

God's generosity is remembered in the Festival of Booths,[4] which commemorates Israel's desert wanderings after leaving Egypt, when Jesus says:

> *Jesus said to them, I am the bread of life; whoever comes to me shall not hunger, and whoever believes in me shall never thirst. (John 6:35)*

The bread here refers to manna and the water refers to God's miraculous gift of water at Meribah (Exod 17:1–17). Reminding temple worshippers of God, Jesus stood up and cried out:

> *If anyone thirsts, let him come to me and drink. Whoever believes in me, as the Scripture has said, Out of his heart will flow rivers of living water.* (John 7:37–39)

The symbolism of water and bread both point to God's abundant and everlasting provision that we commemorate in the sacraments of baptism and communion.

More generally, to *"hunger and thirst for righteousness"* speaks of suffering, where basic human needs are withheld or remain absent, as in songs of lament in the Book of Psalms where we read: *"My God, my God, why have you forsaken me?"* (Ps 22:1) and *"How long, O Lord? Will you hide yourself forever?"*

---

4 John 7:2. An explanation of the Feast of Booths is given in Lev 23:34–43.

(Ps 89:46).[5] It is ironic that God reveals himself most clearly in the deserts of life.[6]

In our deserts of suffering and need, Jesus gives us permission to pray for the simplest needs in life: *"Give us this day our daily bread"* (Matt 6:11), displaying God concern for us.[7] Even in judgment God's eye is on those that care for his people: the righteous are separated from the wicked by their attitude about and care for those in need (Matt 25:31–46).

---

5 Modern atheism feeds from this painful stream. Modern atheists question God's provision and care: if God is all powerful and all good, then the existence of suffering and evil suggests that God is either not all powerful or not good or not both—he does not exist. In contrast, Jesus testifies that those who passionately seek righteousness will be satisfied. The Greek word here for satisfy, χορτάζω, means *"to experience inward satisfaction in something be satisfied"* (BDAG 7954). Far from deserting us, in life Jesus suffered alongside of us, on the cross paid our penalty for sin, and in resurrection became our guarantor. *"While some continue to argue that Auschwitz disproves the existence of God, many more would argue that it demonstrates the depths to which humanity, unrestrained by any thought or fear of God, will sink."* (McGrath 2004, 184).

6 This irony cuts deep. As God tells Moses: *"And you shall say to him [Pharaoh], The LORD, the God of the Hebrews, sent me to you, saying, Let my people go, that they may serve me in the wilderness."* (Exod 7:16) In other words, God was inviting the Israelite people to rediscover the God of their fathers through adversity—this paradox of blessing through adversity must have blown Pharaoh's mind! (Card 2005, 16) After all, the entire sacramental system of the ancient world implicitly associated blessing with bigger sacrifices that only the wealthy could offer.

In contrasting the YHWH economy with Pharaoh's economy, Brueggemann (2009, 31) provides an interesting insight into the Ten Commandments. In the YHWH economy, those who keep the Sabbath need not dishonor mother and father, kill, commit adultery, steal, bear false witness, or covet. In other words, do detestable things for the sake of money. In the unending race to pursue wealth of Pharaoh's economy we are pushed individually and collectively daily to neglect or break these commandments.

7 Even as God expelled Adam and Eve from the Garden of Eden, he clothed them (Gen 3:21).

Our needs will be met and expectations exceeded, we are reminded in the Fourth Beatitude and later in the Sermon on the Mount, when Jesus says:

> *Therefore do not be anxious, saying, What shall we eat? or What shall we drink? or What shall we wear? For the Gentiles seek after all these things, and your heavenly Father knows that you need them all. But seek first the kingdom of God and his righteousness, and all these things will be added to you.* (Matt 6:31–33)

Listen to the phrase—"*seek first the kingdom of God and his righteousness*"—do you hear an echo of the First Commandments? (Exod 20:3) God's righteousness on earth is embedded even in the invitation to share God's peace.

Precious Lord,

In our finitude, our sin, our brokenness, we yearn for your righteousness, oh God. As the hungry grasp for bread and as the thirsty cry for water, we search for your justice where no other will do and no other can be found. Your Holy scriptures remind us that you are ever-near, always vigilant, and forever compassionate. Through the desert of our emotions and in the wilderness of our minds, bind our wounds, relieve our pains, and forgive our sins. Through the power of your Holy Spirit grow our faith even as our strength fails us. In Jesus' precious name, Amen.

Questions
1. What do you hunger and thirst for the most and why?
2. Why is righteousness so elusive?
3. What does the Festival of Booths commemorate?
4. What is God's trademark?
5. What is at the heart of suffering?

4.2: Hunger and Thirst for God

As a deer pants for flowing streams, so pants my soul for you, O God. My soul thirsts for God, for the living God. When shall I come and appear before God? My tears have been my food day and night, while they say to me all the day long, Where is your God? (Ps 42:1–3)

*T*he great irony of faith is that we approach God out of our poverty, not our riches. The riches of Babylon and Egypt flowed from their abundance of water and irrigation systems, while the poverty of Israel blew in with the dust storms from its deserts. Yet, Egypt and Babylon are known for their idolatry and sin, while Israel is known for its law and prophets (Card 2005, 16). What do *the Books of the Law and the Prophets* say about satisfying the hunger and thirst for righteousness?

The Books of the Law. Hungering and thirsting were not part of God's original plan, which we know because food and water were abundant in the Garden of Eden, as we read:

> *And the LORD God planted a garden in Eden, in the east, and there he put the man whom he had formed. And out of the ground the LORD God made to spring up every tree that is pleasant to the sight and good for food. The tree of life was in the midst of the garden, and the tree of the knowledge of good and evil. A river flowed out of Eden to water the garden, and there it divided and became four rivers. (Gen 2:8–10)*

In the Garden of Eden, Adam and Eve lived in direct communion with God and righteousness was a fruit of that communion, which broke down when Adam and Eve sinned (Gen 3:23). When we mourn our sin and the loss of our communion with God, we hunger and thirst for the righteousness, which is a metaphor for the blessings and tangible fruit of that communion.

Restoration of this communion was a goal of the Mosaic covenant, as suggested in Deuteronomy:

> And if you will indeed obey my commandments that I command you today, to love the LORD your God, and to serve him with all your heart and with all your soul, he will give the rain for your land in its season, the early rain and the later rain, that you may gather in your grain and your wine and your oil. And he will give grass in your fields for your livestock, and you shall eat and be full. (Deut 11:13–15)

Obeying the commandments involves loving and serving God, who will respond by sending rain in its season granting you a full harvest and an abundant life for you and yours. By contrast, reluctant service to God will result in servitude, hunger, thirst and deprivation:

> Because you did not serve the LORD your God with joyfulness and gladness of heart, because of the abundance of all things, therefore you shall serve your enemies whom the LORD will send against you, in hunger and thirst, in nakedness,

and lacking everything. And he will put a yoke of iron on your neck until he has destroyed you. (Deut 28:47–48)[1]

Destruction follows from disobedience—under the law one literally reaps what one sows in respect to one's relationship with God. In fact, God's judgment follows from hungering and thirsting for mere physical things, even things like the law (Exod 17:3).[2]

The Books of the Prophets. In the Law, one reaps what one sows; in the Prophets, the wise are clever and the foolish are ignorant of the ways of the world, as we read:

If your enemy is hungry, give him bread to eat, and if he is thirsty, give him water to drink, for you will heap burning coals on his head, and the LORD will reward you. (Prov 25:21–22)

This reward follows for respecting worldly wisdom, because God created both heaven and earth—all knowledge is God's knowledge (Prov 1:7).[3] So the wise leave the door open for enemies to become friends by treating their enemies humanly, feeding them and offering them drink, as Jesus teaches (Matt 5:44–45).

---

1 This theme is repeated over and over (e.g. Deut 8:11–16).

2 This is, in fact, the basis for the curse for not accepting the new covenant in Christ. Paul writes: *"And since they did not see fit to acknowledge God, God gave them up to a debased mind to do what ought not to be done."* (Rom 1:28) To be given over to one's passions is a curse and it leads to self-destruction because both the mind and the heart are corrupted by sin.

3 When Solomon asked God for wisdom to rule the people wisely, God was pleased and granted not only his wish, but also wealth, honor, and a long life (2 Chr 1:10–13).

Feeding and drinking find metaphorical uses in the Prophets, as we read:

> And I will give you shepherds after my own heart, who will feed you with knowledge and understanding. (Jer 3:15)

Jesus himself is this good shepherd (John 10:11–16), but this hunger is relieved metaphorically through *"knowledge and understanding"* rather than through physical consumption. Likewise, mere consumption is not the point when Isaiah alludes to abundant water and food, evoking the image of a return to Eden:

> Come, everyone who thirsts, come to the waters; and he who has no money, come, buy and eat! Come, buy wine and milk without money and without price. Why do you spend your money for that which is not bread, and your labor for that which does not satisfy? Listen diligently to me, and eat what is good, and delight yourselves in rich food. (Isa 55:1–2)

Isaiah offers spiritual water and food which, like their physical counterparts in Eden, were abundantly provided. He infers (as does the Fourth Beatitude) that by hungering and thirsting for righteousness, God will smile on our efforts and heaven will not be far off (Rev 22:17).

Good Shepherd,

We praise you for the gifts of Eden—fertile land, water and food, and the security of your presence. Keep our hands busy; guard our minds; and give us hearts that yearn only for you. Forgive us that we are not fit for Eden; that we are not satisfied with your gifts; that we have not valued your presence; that our hands have been idle, our minds set on physical things, and our hearts easily tempted by crass things. Restore us—make us fit custodians of your garden. Let our hearts yearn for your presence and our minds hunger and thirst for your righteousness, that all the days of our lives our hands may praise you with good works. Through the power of the Holy Spirit and in Jesus' name, Amen.

Questions
1. What is ironic about the wilderness in relation to faith?
2. Did Adam and Eve hunger and thirst in the Garden of Eden?
3. What are some of the blessings and curse of the Mosaic covenant?
4. How do the Books of the Prophets differ from the Books of the Law with respect to hungering and thirsting for God?
5. What kind of leadership and blessings does Isaiah promise?

4.3: Fools for Christ

We are fools for Christ's sake, but you are wise in Christ. We are weak, but you are strong. You are held in honor, but we in disrepute. To the present hour we hunger and thirst, we are poorly dressed and buffeted and homeless, and we labor, working with our own hands. When reviled, we bless; when persecuted, we endure (1 Cor 4:10–12).

W hat are you willing to suffer for? What is your passion?[1]

Apostle Paul's passion was the Gospel and he lived the life of an itinerant evangelist, which means that Paul never married nor had any children (that we know about) and, in spite of being highly educated, gave up a priestly or academic life. When Paul described himself as a fool for Christ (2 Cor 12:10–11), his Jewish parents probably agreed.

Imagine attending your 30th doctoral reunion[2] and rising to address your fellow graduates, saying:

> *I am talking like a madman—with far greater labors, far more imprisonments, with countless beatings, and often near death. Five times I received at the hands of the Jews the forty lashes less one. Three times I was beaten with rods. Once I was stoned. Three times I was shipwrecked; a night and a day I was adrift at sea; on frequent journeys, in danger from rivers, danger from robbers, danger from*

---

1 Jesus said: *"For where your treasure is, there your heart will be also."* (Matt 6:21)

2 The 30th anniversary of my doctorate was December 13, 2015.

my own people, danger from Gentiles, danger in the city, danger in the wilderness, danger at sea, danger from false brothers; in toil and hardship, through many a sleepless night, in hunger and thirst, often without food, in cold and exposure. And, apart from other things, there is the daily pressure on me of my anxiety for all the churches. (2 Cor 11:23–28)

Unlikely to have been church leaders, Paul's classmates were more likely to have been synagogue leaders, high priests, government officials, and college professors. Unlike many of these, Paul hungered and thirsted for righteousness, treating his suffering like a resume, and refused a salary at one point to maintain the integrity of his Gospel message.[3] Like the one who sent him, Paul strived to live life righteously.

Yet, Paul's life of integrity no doubt also put him in tension with God. For example, God's answer to his prayer over a thorn in the flesh—*"My grace is sufficient for you, for my power is made perfect in weakness"* (2 Cor 12:9)—likely caused Paul much anguish before he developed the serenity to boast about God's object lesson.

Another such object lesson is the Eucharist which reminds us of Christ by focusing on objects of hunger (bread) and thirst (water/wine), much like several of Jesus' miracles. Jesus'

3 *"Or did I commit a sin in humbling myself so that you might be exalted, because I preached God's gospel to you free of charge?"* (2 Cor 11:7) Also: *"Do we not have the right to eat and drink?"* (1 Cor 9:4)

first miracle was to turn water into wine (John 2:1–10) while another involved multiplying bread and fish (John 6:11).[4] The transformation of simple things like food and water into sacred objects must have perplexed the Greeks who looked down on the physical world (earth) and looked up to the spiritual world (heaven).

The sacraments and Jesus' miracles point to a simple but important spiritual reality: *"Man shall not live by bread alone."* (Deut 8:3; Luke 4:4) Just as a sacrament is an outward sign with an inward meaning, physical things and circumstances have both outward and inner meanings associated with them, which, for example, leads Paul to describe the body as the temple of God (1 Cor 6:19). If the physical body can become the temple of God and mere food and drink can be sacraments, then food and drink stand at an important boundary between the physical and spiritual realms where spiritual transformation can take place and God's love can be expressed as care for the poor and hungry.

For example, God identifies himself directly with the poor and hungry in the final judgment, as we read:

> *Then the righteous will answer him, saying, Lord, when did we see you hungry and feed you, or thirsty and give you drink? (Matt 25:37)*

---

4 After Jesus' longest recorded discourse with the Samaritan woman about living water, Jesus refers to the word of God as food (John 4:32).

Here, attitude and actions regarding the poor and hungry directly identify Christ's followers, modeled on the charity of Christ himself:

> And he said to me, It is done! I am the Alpha and the Omega, the beginning and the end. To the thirsty I will give from the spring of the water of life without payment. (Rev 21:6)

If Jesus practices charity, then we should be too because our charitable obligation depends, not on the good behavior of the recipients, but on our own identity in Christ:

> if your enemy is hungry, feed him; if he is thirsty, give him something to drink; for by so doing you will heap burning coals on his head. Do not be overcome by evil, but overcome evil with good. (Rom 12:20–21)[5]

Our identity in Christ leads us, not to judge the sinful, but to help the needy, as we read:

> For God did not send his Son into the world to condemn the world, but in order that the world might be saved through him. (John 3:17)

Living in a wealthy nation, our charitable obligation—providing for the physical needs of those less fortunate—is bigger than most.

If the first sin of the Bible was to lust after a tree fruit (Gen 6), then the mark of the disciple would be to model Christ's

---

5 This is the Apostle Paul's paraphrase of Matt 5:43–46.

abundant provision (Rev 21:6) and to defeat the urge to sin.

Almighty Father,

You are the alpha and the omega, the beginning and the end, the one outside of time that created all things. We praise you for providing the bread of life and well-spring of everlasting life which is your son, Jesus Christ—our redeemer, the author of our faith, and our only true friend. We thank you for simple things, like family, bread to eat, clean water to drink, work to do, and friends in Christ. Through the power of your Holy Spirit, help us to share our physical and spiritual gifts with those around us—first our family, then our friends, and even those we do not know well so that your name would be praised among the nations. Forgive us when we play the fool out of pride, not for you, but out of our own ignorance. Humble us that we might become worthy servants of your church and not ourselves. Help us to find our identity in you— not in our friends, nor in our wealth nor in our accomplishments, but in you—so that if we play the fool, it is for you and you alone. In Jesus' precious name, Amen.

Questions
1. What are you willing to suffer for?
2. What was unique about the Apostle Paul's resume?
3. What was the source of Paul's tension with God?
4. If God identifies with the poor and hungry, what does that say to us as Christians?

4.4: In Jesus Completeness is Restored

So God created man in his own image, in the image of God he created him; male and female he created them. (Gen 1:27)

Our tension with God, hungering and thirsting for righteousness, arises out of our incompleteness and separation. Incompletely, we bear God's image in the present age separated by our un-holiness and finitude from our holy and eternal creator. While we remain creatures in God's creation, we are also gardeners expelled from the garden for our sin. Even in our sin, we yearn to be holy; even in our separation, we strive to be reunited.

So in our yearnings and strivings, we have reminders:

Reminders like physical deprivation: an empty stomach hungers; a dry mouth thirsts; a separated individual is lonely.

Reminders like our limitations: dreams forgotten; promises unkept; potential unrealized.

Reminders like spiritual deficits: the times we fall short of the mark; the boundaries that we transgress; the things that we neglect.

So for our sins, transgressions, and neglects, we are thrown out of the garden:

Out of the garden, our energy flags; our hearts and minds feel empty; and pain is our only companion.

Out of the garden, our limits shrink; our cause seems lost; and our destiny beyond reach.

Out of the garden, we feel shame, guilt, and grief; we hear anger, rejection, and accusation; we see ourselves as incomplete, sinful, and unwanted.

In spite of our weaknesses, limitations, and emotions, Jesus offers us a path back to wholeness.

Back to restoration and healing.

Back to the garden and our destiny.

Back to our completeness and holiness and fellowship with our maker.

Jesus said: "Honored are those who hunger and thirst for righteousness, for they shall be satisfied." (Matt 5:6)

Creator God,

We praise you for creating us in your image, complete in ourselves yet complementary with one another. We confess that we have been too quick to sin, and too slow to forgive. Thank you for the gift of Your Son and Our Savior, Jesus Christ. Forgive us; restore us; redeem us—teach us to imitate you so that we might grow more and more like you every day. May we ever hunger and thirst for your righteous presence day by day. Through the power of the Holy Spirit and in Jesus' name, Amen.

Questions
1. How are we incomplete?
2. How are we separated from God?
3. What reminders do we have of our incompleteness, limitations, and spiritual deficits?
4. How do we experience our banishment from the Garden of Eden?
5. What are some attributes of wholeness?

5. HONORED ARE THE MERCIFUL

5.1: JESUS: SHOW MERCY, RECEIVE MERCY

5.2: GOD'S CORE VALUES

5.3: MERCY AS A PATH TO SALVATION

5.4: JESUS MODELS IMAGE ETHICS

5.1: Show Mercy, Receive Mercy

Honored are the merciful, for they shall receive mercy. (Matt 5:7)

*M*ercy highlights our tension with God because our flesh delights neither in practicing mercy nor in offering it. Rather than practice mercy, we prefer people to keep their promises and pay their bills; rather than ask for mercy, we prefer to pretend that we are sinless. Born in sin, mercy draws attention to our lack of holiness and our finitude, highlighting our tension with God.

Mercy is one of God's signature character traits,[1] appearing in the Golden Rule, in the Lord's Prayer, and, most significantly, in a short list of God's attributes given to Moses immediately after the Ten Commandments on Mount Sinai:

> *The LORD passed before him and proclaimed, The LORD, the LORD, a God merciful and gracious, slow to anger, and abounding in steadfast love and faithfulness, keeping steadfast love for thousands, forgiving iniquity and transgression and sin, but who will by no means clear the guilty, visiting the iniquity of the fathers on the children and the children's children, to the third and the fourth generation.* (Exod 34:6–7)

The Sinai context here is important because God exposes his

1 *"Mercy is a central biblical theme, because in God's great mercy he does not give humans what they deserve, rather, he gives to them what they do not deserve . . ."* (Wilkins 2004, 208). Mercy is mentioned about 30 times in the Old Testament and in all but 4 times God's mercy is in view (Guelich 1982, 88).

character traits to Moses as a set of core values to be used to interpret the law correctly. Experienced lawmakers know that laws taken out of context can be misinterpreted and they frequently publish commentaries to assure proper interpretation. To interpret God's character correctly, start by recognizing that God is merciful. God demonstrates his mercy in that Jesus willingly died on the cross to save us from our sins—our atonement through Christ confirms his divinity precisely because it exemplifies God's mercy (1 Cor 15:3).

Mercy appears in many grammatical forms in scripture, but the adverbial form (ἐλεήμονες; *"elehmones"*)[2] used in the Fifth Beatitude is used nowhere else. Merciful (ἐλεήμων; *"elehmon"*) means *"being concerned about people in their need, merciful, sympathetic, compassionate"*.[3] Mercy (ἔλεος; *"eleos"*) has the same root as compassion (ἐλεημοσύνη; *"elehmosune"*) and is closely related to forgive (ἀφίημι; *"hafimi"*). Mercy and forgiveness are two sides of the same coin,[4] as we read:

> *Remember your mercy, O LORD, and your steadfast love, for they have been from of old. Remember not the sins of my youth or my transgressions; according to your steadfast love remember me, for the sake of your goodness, O LORD!* (Ps 25:6–7)

2 Wallace (1996, 460–461) describes the adverbial form as having two interpretations. It is either declarative or causal. Here it appears to be causal.
3 (BDAG 2487).
4 See: Guelich (1982, 88).

The Psalmist talks about mercy, love, and goodness, which together constitute forgiveness.

Jesus repeatedly talks about mercy, as when we read:

> 1. *Go and learn what this means, I desire mercy, and not sacrifice.*[5] *For I came not to call the righteous, but sinners.* (Matt 9:13)[6]

> 2. *Woe to you, scribes and Pharisees, hypocrites! For you tithe mint and dill and cumin, and have neglected the weightier matters of the law: justice and mercy and faithfulness. These you ought to have done, without neglecting the others.* (Matt 23:23)

> 3. *And should not you have had mercy on your fellow servant, as I had mercy on you?* (Matt 18:33)

Jesus clearly values mercy more than legal compliance or punishment. He also talks about mercy using other words or phrases, as in:

> 1. *So whatever you wish that others would do to you, do also to them, for this is the Law and the Prophets.* (Matt 7:12)

> 2. *Forgive us our debts, as we also have forgiven our debtors.* (Matt 6:12)

In the first example of the *Golden Rule*, he uses the reciprocal form[7] (do as you would have them do) also used in the Fifth Be-

---

5 Hos 6:6.

6 Also: Matt 12:7.

7 See: (France 1985,110).

atitude (give mercy, receive mercy) suggesting through parallel construction that a parallel concept is also being discussed.

The reciprocal form of the Fifth Beatitude makes a convincing case for mercy. Mercy is not earned by being merciful, but mercy suggests God's presence and we are blessed when we offer it.

God of All Compassion and Mercy,

Forgive me, Lord, for the sins of my youth when I fell short of the plans you had for me. When in your great compassion you were kind to me and patient, teaching me your law and demonstrating your grace. Forgive me, Lord, for the transgressions of my youth when I disobeyed your law when in your mercy you looked the other way and disregarded my attitude, teaching me forbearance and gentle persuasion. Forgive me, Lord, for the iniquity of my youth when I failed to help those around me. When in your everlasting love you sent your son to die to me, atoning for my sin, my transgressions, and my iniquity so that I might grow to be a man mindful of compassion, mercy, and love that were modeled for me all the days of my life. In Jesus' precious name, Amen.

✿

Questions
1. How do we know about God's mercy?
2. What words are used to express God's mercy in the Bible?
3. Why might mercy be called God's signature character trait? What examples can be given?
4. What are God's core values?

5.2: God's Core Values

The LORD passed before him [Moses] and proclaimed, The LORD, the LORD, a God merciful and gracious, slow to anger, and abounding in steadfast love and faithfulness, keeping steadfast love for thousands, forgiving iniquity and transgression and sin, but who will by no means clear the guilty, visiting the iniquity of the fathers on the children and the children's children, to the third and the fourth generation. (Exod 34:6–7)

*I*mmediately following the giving of the Ten Commandments, God proclaims his attributes to Moses, much like a herald might introduce the titles and accomplishments of an important dignitary. Scripture underscores the importance of these attributes by repeating them, almost word for word, in Psalm 86:15 and Psalm 103:8, Joel 2:13, and Jonah 4:2. In the parallel context of the giving of the Law (Deut 4:31), only mercy is cited, underscoring its primacy in the Jewish understanding of God's character.

The emphasis on mercy and the de-emphasis on faithfulness (or truth) in these passages suggests that God is soft-hearted. Exodus 34:6 mentions mercy (רַחוּם; *"rahum"*), gracious (חַנּוּן; *"hannun"*), slow to anger (אֶרֶךְ אַפַּיִם; *"erek apayim"*)[1], abounding in love (רַב־חֶסֶד; *"rav hesed"*)[2], and faithfulness (אֱמֶת; *"emeth"*)

---

1 Or long nostrilled.

2 Hesed love is best translated as *"covenantal love"* because of the context here as God just delivered the Ten Commandments to Moses. When we get married, we hope to be romantic but bank on our spouse keeping their promises.

[3]and Psalm 86:15 repeats each of the five words in the same order. Psalm 103 repeats the first four words, but drops faithfulness. Joel 2:13 repeats the first five words, but substitutes *"relents over disaster"* for faithfulness. Jonah 4:2 likewise substitutes *"relents over disaster"* for faithfulness but swaps grace and mercy. The emphasis on mercy and the de-emphasis on faithfulness in God's attributes is important because they provide guidance on how to interpret law especially when conflicts arise or when a new context requires interpretation.[4]

The primacy of mercy in the Jewish understanding of God's character figures prominently in the story of Jonah, who refused God's call to preach repentance to the sinful people of Nineveh[5] and, rather than answer God's call, boarded a ship going the opposite direction (Jonah 1:2–3). After being caught in a storm, thrown overboard, and rescued by a whale, Jonah reluctantly responded to God's call, traveled to Nineveh, and preached repentance to the Ninevites. When the Ninevites responded to

3 *"Emeth"* is often translated as faithfulness, but it also means truth. For this reason, when the Apostle John writes that— *"And the Word became flesh and dwelt among us, and we have seen his glory, glory as of the only Son from the Father, full of grace and truth. "* (John 1:14)—the reference to *"grace and truth"* is a claim that Jesus is God and Exodus 34:6 is directly in view.

4 Law has the benefit of being concrete establishing specific principles which are the focus of the field of theology (the study of the nature of God). But in application circumstances are often messy bringing these principles into conflict which is focus the field of ethics (the study of right and wrong action).

5 The Book of Nahum is an oracle against Nineveh specifically (Nahum 1:1). The city's ruins lie across the Tigris River from Mosul in modern Iraq.

his preaching, turned from their sin, and begged God to forgive them (Jonah 3:9–10), God relented from destroying the city of Nineveh and, in response to God's mercy, Jonah got angry.

Showing mercy to Nineveh probably seemed unjust to Jonah and made him angry, because Nineveh was the hometown of Sennacherib, king of Assyria who conquered Judah and made King Hezekiah his vassal,[6] so Jonah:

> prayed to the LORD and said, O LORD, is not this what I said when I was yet in my country? That is why I made haste to flee to Tarshish; for I knew that you are a gracious God and merciful, slow to anger and abounding in steadfast love, and relenting from disaster. (Jonah 4:2)

Jonah knew God's attributes (citing Exod 34:6) and did not want to give the hated Ninevites the opportunity to repent and have God forgive them, as he knew God in his mercy would.[7]

Mercy is first among God's attributes because as human beings we are born in sin and must acknowledge our sin before we feel any need for God. Our need is like that of a young man who, not liking the newly elected president, leaves the country, and tears up his passport; without being issued a new passport, he cannot return home. In our case, our passport into the king-

---

6 See: (2 Kgs 19:36; Isa 37:37) and (Isa 36:2).

7 When we refuse to share the Good News of Jesus Christ with our neighbors, we become like Jonah selfishly trying to keep God's mercy to ourselves—evidence of the continuing influence of the fall in our own lives.

dom of God is his mercy, without which we cannot experience God's other attributes.

Merciful God,

I praise you for the gift of your law and your provision of grace through Jesus Christ that we might approach you in prayer. You are the God of mercy and grace, who is slow to anger, abounding in love, and faithful. There is none like you; may I ever model myself on your immutable character remembering your law, being ever-mindful of your grace, and enjoying the support of your church. May I be quick to share your mercy, grace, and love with those around me in thought, word, and deed through the power of the Holy Spirit, and in Jesus' name, Amen.

Questions
1. What are God's attributes? What is the relationship between God's attributes and law?
2. Where is Nineveh and why are the Ninevites famous?
3. Why did Jonah run away when God told him to go to Nineveh? How did his decision relate to God's attributes?
4. Who are the Ninevites in your life? How do you feel when

God offers them mercy?

5. How do you experience God's love?

5.3: Mercy as a Path to Salvation

Go and learn what this means, I desire mercy, and not sacrifice.
For I came not to call the righteous, but sinners. (Matt 9:13)

*A*sking for mercy and offering mercy both evoke tension with God because we prefer not to shine a light on our own sin or the sin of others. In dealing with our own sin, Jesus cites the same verse from the Prophet Hosea twice[1] after the Fifth Beatitude:

> For I desire steadfast love[2] and not sacrifice, the knowledge of God rather than burnt offerings. (Hos 6:6)

Pagan worship attempts to manipulate the gods with sacrifices, which today can take the form of offerings, overt righteousness, prayers, church attendance, or XYZ actions done, not out of thanksgiving, but out of a desire to manipulate God.

An important lesson on mercy shows up the story of the Good Samaritan when a lawyer asks Jesus, *"And who is my neighbor?"* (Luke 10:29)[3]. After telling the story, Jesus asks,*"Which of these three, do you think, proved to be a neighbor to the man*

---

1 Matt 9:13 and 12:7.

2 There is tension in the Greek and Hebrew texts on this word, translated here as steadfast love. The Greek reads mercy (ἔλεος) and the Hebrew reads love (דֶסֶח). The citations in Matt 9:13 and 12:7 go with the Greek. The translation of Hos 6:6 in the English Standard Version (ESV) goes with the Hebrew.

3 Luke 10:25–28.

who fell among the robbers?" (Luke 10:36), substituting the question—*"who proved to be a neighbor"*—for the lawyer's question—*"who is my neighbor"*—and eliciting the lawyer's response—*"The one who showed him mercy."* (Luke 10:37) Notice how the story started out talking about neighborly love, but ended up talking about mercy?[4]

Mercy is a fitting focus of the story of the Good Samaritan because Jews hated Samaritans and the Samaritan had to overcome prejudice (show mercy) in order to show love to the man left for dead—in the same way, we experience God's love through his mercy, as in this verse:

> *The LORD, the LORD, a God merciful and gracious, slow to anger, and abounding in steadfast love and faithfulness* (Exod 34:6)

Notice that this verse includes both mercy and love, but mercy comes first.

James draws a parallel conclusion from God's attributes when he observes:

> *For judgment is without mercy to one who has shown no mercy. Mercy triumphs over judgment.* (Jas 2:13)[5]

---

4 A more typical sermon focuses on neighborliness. By turning a direct object (neighbor) into a verb (to be a neighbor) Jesus redirects the lawyer's question from who can be excluded as a neighbor to how we can become a better neighbor.

5 In the citation above, James has restated Jesus' Beatitude in the negative—it

Judgment requires truth (אֱמֶת; *"emeth"*),[6] which—like love—follows mercy on the list of God's attributes.

The link between judgment and mercy points us back to the atoning work of Christ, as the Apostle Peter observed:

> Blessed be the God and Father of our Lord Jesus Christ! According to his great mercy, he has caused us to be born again to a living hope through the resurrection of Jesus Christ from the dead, to an inheritance that is imperishable, undefiled, and unfading, kept in heaven for you, who by God's power are being guarded through faith for a salvation ready to be revealed in the last time. (1 Pet 1:3–5)

The path to salvation through Christ is by way of his mercy.

Merciful Father, Beloved Son, Ever-present Spirit,

We praise you, Lord, for your mercy, grace, patience, love, and faithfulness; for healing us of our afflictions, for forgiving our sin, and for your presence in our life; for in you we find faith, hope, and love, as nowhere else. We confess that you alone are God, yet we make idols of machines, institutions, and our own pet theories. We have not followed the example of your son, Jesus

---

is a curse to be judged without mercy.

6 As cited above, the use of *"emeth"* in Exod 34:6 is often translated also as faithfulness.

Christ, and have set our own desires above our families, friends, and even your church. Forgive our sin; overlook our transgressions; and heal us of our iniquity—that we might be whole again and restored to your presence. We give thanks for the many blessings that you have freely given us: our families, our health, our work, and even life itself. We ask you now to bless us that we might bless others. In Jesus' name, Amen.

Questions
1. Why is mercy an unpopular divine attribute?
2. What is paganism's defining characteristic and why do the prophets de-emphasize the sacrifice system?
3. What is the relationship between mercy and love?
4. Why does the Bible stress mercy over love and truth?

5.4: Jesus Models Image Ethics

So Jesus said to them, Truly, truly, I say to you, the Son can do nothing of his own accord, but only what he sees the Father doing. For whatever the Father does, that the Son does likewise. (John 5:19)

*T*he creation account in Genesis offers an ethical framework which Jesus employs repeatedly in his teaching. In Genesis, we read:

> *So God created man in his own image, in the image of God he created him; male and female he created them.* (Gen 1:27)

Because we are created in the image of God, our behavior should likewise follow God's behavior—a kind of *image ethic*. For example, when God blesses us, we should bless others (Gen 12:3). This behavioral pattern is simple—God does A, we do A; God does B, we do B—and this pattern appears several places in Jesus' teachings, such as in the Lord's Prayer where we read:

> *Your kingdom come, your will be done, on earth as it is in heaven.* (Matt 6:10)

The phrase *"on earth as it is in heaven"* models this pattern while the phrase—*"and forgive us our debts, as we also have forgiven our debtors"* (Matt 6:12)—reverses the pattern because we know God's will.

In discussing forgiveness, Jesus pauses to repeat himself,

for emphasis:

> *For if you forgive others their trespasses, your heavenly Father will also forgive you, but if you do not forgive others their trespasses, neither will your Father forgive your trespasses.* (Matt 6:14–15)

In six simple verses (Matt 6:10–15), Jesus repeats this reversal pattern (we do A, God does A; we do B, God does B,) four times when God's will is well known (God is merciful so he obviously forgives), as when God's character traits inform us.

Accordingly, an important application of this pattern is to reflect and anticipate all of God character traits:[1]

> *…The LORD, the LORD, a God merciful and gracious, slow to anger, and abounding in steadfast love and faithfulness…* (Exod 34:6)

If God is merciful, then we are merciful; if God is gracious, we are gracious . . . Among the fruits of the Spirit, the Apostle Paul lists:

> *love, joy, peace, patience, kindness, goodness, faithfulness, gentleness, self-control; against such things there is no law.* (Gal 5:22–23)

Almost all of God's character traits are found on this list, albeit kindness only hints at mercy.

---

1 Billy Graham read this Beatitude a bit more concretely. He wrote: *"What are some of the areas in today's world toward which we can show mercy? First: We can show mercy by caring for the social needs of our fellow men…Second: We can show mercy by doing away with our prejudices…Third: We can show mercy by sharing the gospel of Christ with others."* (Graham 1955, 61–65).

Do you want a blessing? Be a blessing![2]

Simple. Clean. Convicting.

Jesus loves image ethics.

God of all mercy and grace,

We praise you for creating the heaven and the earth, all that is, that was, and that will ever be; all things seen and unseen. We look upon your creation, smile, and praise your name. We praise you for the example of your son, our savior, Jesus Christ—who in life served others, who in death atoned for our sin, and who in rising from the dead granted us the hope of eternal life. We see your son's example and feel your love for us. We praise you for your Holy Spirit, who draws us to you, grants every good gift, and provides all things. We look upon your Holy Spirit's power in the world and break out in praise. May your kingdom come, your will be done, on earth as it is in heaven, today and every day, with us and through us. In Jesus' name, Amen.

---

2 One is reminded here of Abraham's blessing: *"And I will make of you a great nation, and I will bless you and make your name great, so that you will be a blessing."* (Gen 12:2)

Questions
1. Who is our model for ethical behavior?
2. What is the pattern? Where does Jesus repeat the pattern? Where does Jesus deviate from the pattern?
3. How do you interpret Genesis 12:2 in view of this pattern?
4. What does it mean to be created in the image of God? What attribute(s) of God is (are) in view here?
5. What does it mean to be created male and female in the image of God?

6. HONORED ARE THE PURE IN HEART

6.1: BE HOLY FOR I AM HOLY

6.2: A RIGHT SPIRIT AND CLEAN HEART

6.3: PRUNE, INTENSIFY, AND APPLY

6.4: LIVING INTO OUR CALL

6.1: Be Holy For I am Holy

Honored are the pure in heart, for they shall see God. (Matt 5:8)

G od is holy; we are not. Our tension with God often starts with guilt over this holiness gap. This gap, which is more of a chasm, points to our need for Christ, who is our bridge to our Holy God.[1]

The Greek word for pure (καθαρός; *"catharos"*) means: *"to be free from moral guilt, pure, free from sin"*.[2] The expression pure in heart (καθαρὸς τῇ καρδίᾳ; *"catharos te cardia"*) appears only in Matthew 5:8 in the New Testament but occurs in the Old Testament:

> *Who shall ascend the hill of the LORD? And who shall stand in his holy place? He who has clean hands and a pure heart, who does not lift up his soul to what is false and does not swear deceitfully.* (Ps 24:3–4)

This Psalm tells us how to worship in the temple in Jerusalem. In view is the holiness code of Leviticus where God admonishes us many times to *"be holy, for I am holy"* (Lev 11:44).

The expression, *"pure in heart"*, is incomplete in the English translation. The Hebrew word for heart (לֵב; *"lev"*) means

---

1 The exclusiveness of Christ occurs because he is both God and man which is a necessity for bridging both the holiness gap and the gap between mortal and immortal beings.

2 (BDAG 3814 (3c)).

"inner man, mind, will, heart"[3] which includes emotions but also things not included in the English. For example, immediately following the Hebrew prayer, the Shema,[4] we are commanded—*"You shall love the LORD your God with all your heart and with all your soul and with all your might."* (Deut 6:5)—which emphasizes this point (heart, soul, might) through repetition.[5] Jesus repeats this reference in Matthew 22:36–40 where he commands us to love both God and our neighbor.[6]

The Sixth Beatitude's promise of seeing God, if we remain pure, is also a promise of forgiveness (Ps 51:10–12), salvation (Job 19:26–27), and the opportunity of ministry. Seeing God figures prominently in the call stories of Moses (Exod 3:6), Isaiah (Isa 6:5), and Ezekiel (Ezek 1:28) whose experience parallels that of Paul[7] who is blinded by the light of heaven (an allusion to God).[8] As unholy and mortal beings, seeing God blinds us and

3 (BDB 4761).

4 *"Hear, O Israel: The LORD our God, the LORD is one."* (Deut 6:4)

5 The unity of heart and mind (or body, soul, and mind) implies that having a pure heart is a holistic statement of purity—purity throughout our entire person or being. Benner (1998, 22) notes that when the Bible refers to a division of the person, the division is for emphasis, not to infer that the person can be divided into separate and distinct parts.

6 Love God; love neighbor.

7 Paul's conversion and call experience is repeated three times in the Book of Acts: Acts 9:3, 22:6, and 26:13.

8 The Acts 26 allusion to Ezekiel is the most complete: "ἀνάστηθι καὶ στῆθι ἐπὶ τοὺς πόδας" (arise and stand on your feet; Acts 26:16 BNT) which compares with Ezekiel's words: "στῆθι ἐπὶ τοὺς πόδας" (stand on your feet; Ezek 2:1 BGT)

threatens our very existence.

The promise of seeing God is also a promise of restoration of the relationship with God, seen first in the Garden of Eden (Gen 3:8–9). It also anticipates heaven, as prophesied in the last chapter of the Book of Revelation:

> No longer will there be anything accursed, but the throne of God and of the Lamb will be in it, and his servants will worship him. They will see his face, and his name will be on their foreheads. (Rev 22:3–4)

Holiness is the mark of God, not only on our foreheads, but also on our souls, as we read in Genesis:

> Now Abimelech had not approached her. So he said, Lord, will you kill an innocent people? Did he not himself say to me, She is my sister'? And she herself said, He is my brother. In the integrity of my heart and the innocence of my hands I have done this. Then God said to him in the dream, Yes, I know that you have done this in the integrity of your heart, and it was I who kept you from sinning against me. Therefore I did not let you touch her. (Gen 20:4–6)

Abimelech speaks directly with God who works in his heart to keep him from sinning.

Seeing Jesus, a *"friend of . . . sinners"*,[9] value and teach

---

9 *For John the Baptist has come eating no bread and drinking no wine, and you say, He has a demon. The Son of Man has come eating and drinking, and you say, Look at him! A glutton and a drunkard, a friend of tax collectors and sinners! Yet wisdom is justified by all her children.* (Luke 7:33–35)

about holiness is indeed ironic, but the Sixth Beatitude anticipates our conversion and commissioning, much like that of the Apostles:

> *As the Father has sent me, even so I am sending you. And when he had said this, he breathed on them and said to them, Receive the Holy Spirit.* (John 20:21–22).

The call of an Apostle clearly required a purity of heart which the Holy Spirit brought within their reach.

Holy and Eternal Father,

We praise you for your mercy and grace through Jesus Christ, who died for our sins before we were even born. We confess that you alone are holy. From our mother's womb we have tried your patience and even now come to you with blood stained hands. Forgive us in our rebellion against your covenant and against your son. In the power of your Holy Spirit, cleanse our hearts and minds that we might become fit stewards of your mercy and grace to those among us who have not heard the good news or have rejected it on account of our sin and folly. Draw us to yourself today across the gaps that separate us that we might have new life in you, this day, and forever more. In Jesus' precious name, Amen.

Questions
1. What is our first source of tension with God?
2. What does it mean to be pure in heart?
3. What is the Shema and why is it important in understanding God's love?
4. What is the double love command?
5. What is promised in the Sixth Beatitude? Why?
6. Why is God's holiness a potential threat?
7. Who is Abimelch? Why is God's intervention in his life interesting?

6.2: A Right Spirit and Clean Heart

Create in me a clean heart, O God, and renew a right spirit within me. Cast me not away from your presence, and take not your Holy Spirit from me. (Ps 51:10–11)

When we think of the word, *"holy"*, we usually think of moral purity, but another definition is: *"pertaining to being dedicated or consecrated to [set apart to] the service of God".*[1] The same word for holy in Greek (ἅγιος; *"hagios"*) also means saint, as well as morally pure and separate.

Moral purity and separation are fundamental ideas in the Old Testament understanding of God, as seen in Genesis: *"In the beginning, God created the heavens and the earth."* (Gen 1:1) Two acts of separation occur in creation: non-being is separated from being (Gen 1:1a) and the heavens and the earth are separated from one another (Gen 1:1b). Other separations—darkness and light, morning and evening, dry land and water, male and female—follow in the creation account which God declares to be good.[2]

Good separations, often referred to today as boundaries, need to be clear and concrete. In the Ten Commandments (Exod

1 (BDAG 61).

2 Contemporary attacks on the goodness of God often start by declaring these separations arbitrary and capricious, especially as they pertain to questions of gender. The argument goes that if these separations are arbitrary, they are also discriminatory, hence not good. Therefore, the Bible teaches discrimination and cannot be considered normative for postmodern Christians.

20), the law sets forth voluntary boundaries defining who is and is not part of the household of God. This covenant between the people of Israel and God begins with a reminder of the benefits of the covenant: *"I am the LORD your God, who brought you out of the land of Egypt, out of the house of slavery."* (Exod 20:2) In other words, you were once slaves, but I set you free.[3]

The covenantal benefits (blessings) and strictures (curses) were laid out in greater detail in Deuteronomy,[4] where we first read about the benefits:

> *And if you faithfully obey the voice of the Lord your God, being careful to do all his commandments that I command you today, the Lord your God will set you high above all the nations of the earth. And all these blessings shall come upon you and overtake you, if you obey the voice of the Lord your God. Blessed shall you be in the city, and blessed shall you be in the field....* (Deut 28:1–3)

Later in parallel fashion, we read about the strictures:

> *But if you will not obey the voice of the Lord your God or be careful to do all his commandments and his statutes that I command you today, then all these curses shall come upon you and overtake you. Cursed shall you be in the city, and cursed shall you*

3 The Apostle Paul talks about being a slave to sin (Rom 7:14). Today we talk about slavery to an addiction, being slaves to fear, or slaves to other passions. The point of Exod 20:2 is that God offers us the freedom to escape such bondage, if we seek him.

4 Deuteronomy, which means the second book of the law, needed to repeat the covenant for a new generation because God cursed their parents (who had lived in Egypt) for their lack of faith to die in the desert (Deut 1:20–37).

be in the field... (Deut 28:15–16)

These blessings and curses are cited again in Psalm 1:

> *Blessed is the man who walks not in the counsel of the wicked, nor stands in the way of sinners, nor sits in the seat of scoffers...* (Ps 1:1)

Reminding people, especially leaders, of these blessings and curses was the primary responsibility of an Old Testament prophet. Those that kept their covenantal obligations were considered righteous under the law (Phil 3:6).

If God considered Job righteous, then why did Job end up suffering? (Job 1:1)

One response to the question of suffering is that Job's faithfulness was tested by evil circumstances (Job 1:9) and confirmed to be true (Job 42:1–7). Another response is that suffering is a consequence of foolishness (Prov 1:7). The best response is that sin brings suffering, is part of our nature, and God's intervention is required to overcome it, as we read:

> *For I know that my Redeemer lives, and at the last he will stand upon the earth. And after my skin has been thus destroyed, yet in my flesh I shall see God, whom I shall see for myself, and my eyes shall behold, and not another...* (Job 19:25–27)

This theodicy of Job reveals God's glory and his love for us in providing us a redeemer.

The possibility of a redeemer is prophesied by Moses

(Deut 18:15) and is an expression of God's forgiveness (Exod 34:7). In praying for God's forgiveness, King David expressed most clearly God's intervention in our moral condition:

> Create in me a clean heart, O God, and renew a
> right spirit within me. Cast me not away from your
> presence, and take not your Holy Spirit from me.
> (Ps 51:10–11)

David recognized that divine intervention was required for a human relationship with a holy and transcendent God.[5]

Later, God intervened through the death and resurrection of Jesus Christ to atone for our sin (1 Cor 15:3–10). In Christ and through the Holy Spirit, we can live in obedience to God (set free from the law) and can come before God in prayer and worship.

Father of Creation, Beloved Son, Spirit of Truth,

Bind our wayward hearts with your law; sing to us of your love. Gather our confused thoughts in your grace; center them on your truth. Separate us from evil influences, harsh temptations, and trials we cannot bear. Walk with us when

---

5 To be human means to be unholy and mortal, not holy and immortal (transcendent), like God.

the sun fails to shine, the rain draws near, and our paths become unclear. Sit with us while storms rage, our strength weakens, and our health flees. Guide us when our friends are distant and our troubles are ever near. Grant us strength for the day; grace for those we meet; and peace. In Jesus' name, Amen.

Questions
1. What are two implications of the word, holy?
2. What is a separation or boundary? What kind of separations do we find in the Bible?
3. What do blessings and curses have to do with the Ten Commandments?
4. What is the primary job description of an Old Testament prophet?
5. Why is a redeemer needed in the Old Testament? What does redemption have to do with law?
6. What role does Christ play in our redemption?

6.3: Prune, Intensify, and Apply

You have heard that it was said, You shall not commit adultery. But I say to you that everyone who looks at a woman with lustful intent has already committed adultery with her in his heart. If your right eye causes you to sin, tear it out and throw it away. For it is better that you lose one of your members than that your whole body be thrown into hell. (Matt 5:27–29)

The Sixth Beatitude focuses on a clean heart—*"Honored are the pure in heart"*—but, how can I remove the impurities? Jesus provides three methods: pruning, intensifying, and applying.

Prune. Jesus gives us two metaphors of pruning—cutting away unnecessary or unwanted growth to make a plant stronger and more fruitful (John 15:2). The first metaphor involves eyes: *"If your right eye causes you to sin, tear it out and throw it away."* (Matt 5:29) The second metaphor involves hands: *"And if your right hand causes you to sin, cut it off and throw it away."* (Matt 5:30) In both metaphors, we remove sin from our lives by pruning.[1]

---

1 The eye gouging and hand chopping metaphors could also have been heard by Jesus' audience as a messianic call to arms. When the Prophet Samuel anointed Saul messianic king of Israel, he said to him: *"And you shall reign over the people of the LORD and you will save them from the hand of their surrounding enemies."* (1 Sam 10:1) Notice the hand metaphor in this charge. Saul's first act as king was to save the besieged city of Jabesh-gilead from an Amorite king whose condition for surrender was: *"On this condition I will make a treaty with you, that I gouge out all your right eyes, and thus bring disgrace on all Israel."* (1 Sam 11:2) Understanding the story of Saul, Jesus' metaphors might be interpreted as saying: stand on your own two feet.

Jesus' pruning metaphors imply that sanctification—casting off sin and taking on godliness—is serious business: eyes and hands are parts of the body—parts of us—that are not easily discarded. If the threat of sin were trivial, then a better analogy might have been to trim your nails or cut your hair. But if sin threatens both our physical and spiritual lives, then amputation is an acceptable option and the analogy is not hyperbolic.

Intensify. Jesus widens the scope of commandments under the law by drilling into the motivation for breaking them, intensifying the scrutiny given to sin. For example, when Jesus talks about adultery, he focuses on the lustful look that corrupts the heart, not the sinful act that follows.[2] If sin begins in the heart, then sanctification must strive for purity of heart, and not only avoiding sin, but pursuing godliness, as the Apostle Paul writes:

> *But that is not the way you learned Christ!—assuming that you have heard about him and were taught in him, as the truth is in Jesus, to put off your old self, which belongs to your former manner of life and is corrupt through deceitful desires, and to be renewed in the spirit of your minds, and to put on the new self, created after the likeness of God in true righteousness and holiness.* (Eph 4:20–24)

The likeness of God, of course, refers to the divine image in cre-

---

2 As evangelist Billy Graham reminds us: *"What does this word adultery mean? It is derived from the same Latin root from which we get our word adulterate which means corrupt; to make impure or to weaken."* (Graham 1955, 78).

ation, as implied in the word, godliness, used by Paul in admonishing Timothy: *"train yourself for godliness"* (1 Tim 4:7).

Apply. In the Jewish mindset, it makes no sense to separate heart and mind or faith from action,[3] as we read in James:

> *But be doers of the word, and not hearers only, deceiving yourselves. For if anyone is a hearer of the word and not a doer, he is like a man who looks intently at his natural face in a mirror. For he looks at himself and goes away and at once forgets what he was like. But the one who looks into the perfect law, the law of liberty, and perseveres, being no hearer who forgets but a doer who acts, he will be blessed in his doing.* (Jas 1:22–25)

As a devote Jew, James would almost certainly share Jesus' conviction that unity of person (heart and mind) implies unity of faith and action.[4] In fact, the gap between what we say and what we do is a good measure of the amount of sin in our lives. After all, Jesus was the first person in scripture to use the word, *"hypocrite"*, to mean *"two-faced"*—saying one thing and doing another.[5] Prior to Jesus, an hypocrite was just an actor on a Greek stage.

---

3 To pursue holiness and to practice godliness the heart and mind must work together to unify the person. Bridges (1996a, 7) writes: *"The Pursuit of Holiness [his earlier book title] dealt largely with putting off the old self—dealing with sin in our lives. The Practice of Godliness [his later book title] focuses on putting on the new self—growing in Christian character."*

4 This unity of faith and action also extends to inanimate objects. For the Hebrew, beauty extends not only to appearance but also to function (Dyrness 2001, 81).

5 *"Woe to you, scribes and Pharisees, hypocrites! For you clean the outside of the cup and the plate, but inside they are full of greed and self-indulgence."* (Matt

Unity of faith and action is, of course, a divine attribute, as we see in the life and work of Jesus Christ. In life, Jesus modeled God's sinless nature for us (Heb 4:15); in death, Jesus redeemed us from our sin (Gal 3:13); in resurrection, Jesus gave us the hope of salvation (1 Cor 15:20); and, in ascension, intercedes for us before Almighty God (Rev 22:3). Following the ascension at Pentecost, Jesus conferred on the church and on us the Holy Spirit to assist us in overcoming our sinful nature (John 16:7–8).

So when we act in unity of faith and action, we echo the Trinity:

> *Hear, O Israel: The LORD our God, the LORD is one. You shall love the LORD your God with all your heart and with all your soul and with all your might.* (Deut 6:4–5)

In this manner, we model God's sinless nature to those around us. Modeling Christ, we must prune, intensify, and apply if we are to be pure in heart and see God.

Almighty Father.

Spare us, Lord, from a divided heart, an indecisive mind, and conniving spirit. Prune the eye that sins, the hand that grasps,

23:25)

and the ears that itch to hear anything other than your word. Intensify our love of your law and apply that love in gracious hearts and discerning minds. Instill in us your Holy Spirit, holy affections, and sanctified thoughts that we might be truthful to ourselves, to others, and, most of all, to you. Grant us your whole armor: the belt of truth, the breastplate of righteousness, helmet of salvation, and sword of your word (Eph 6:13–17). That we might serve our entire lives as examples of your godliness. In Jesus' name, Amen.

Questions
1. What are three methods for obtaining a clean heart?
2. Where does Jesus get the idea of pruning? Why is it helpful?
3. What does it mean to intensify? How would you describe the pursuit of godliness?
4. Can faith and action be separated? What is a hypocrite and what did it mean originally?
5. Can we be faithful on our own?

6.4: Living into Our Call

The earth is the LORD's and the fullness thereof, the world and those who dwell therein, for he has founded it upon the seas and established it upon the rivers. Who shall ascend the hill of the LORD? And who shall stand in his holy place? He who has clean hands and a pure heart, who does not lift up his soul to what is false and does not swear deceitfully. (Ps 24:1–4)

Sometimes decreasing tension with a holy God means increasing our tension with the world. In David Kinnaman and Gabe Lyons' recent book, *UnChristian*, the six most common points of tension between Christians and non-Christians were:

> 1. Hypocritical. *We say one thing and do another.*
>
> 2. Christians are: *"too focused on getting converts."*
>
> 3. Homophobic. *"Christians are bigoted and show distain for gays and lesbians."*
>
> 4. Sheltered. Christians are: *"old-fashioned, boring, and out of touch with reality".*
>
> 5. Too political. Christians: *"promote and represent politically conservative interests and issues."*
>
> 6. Judgmental. People doubt that *"we really love people as we say we do."* (Kinnaman 2007, 29–30).

Non-Christian doubts about Christian holiness lie behind each of these criticisms. For example, Christians who act like everyone else—especially in matters of sexuality—are rightly seen as hypocritical, not holy. By contrast, Christians who pursue holiness may make some others feel uncomfortably judged, eliciting unfair criticism and well-earned tension.

When holiness issues are raised within the church, discussion is often cut off with a question—where is the grace in your worldview? In view here is the presumed tension between grace and law in the Gospel of John:

> For from his fullness we have all received, grace upon grace. For the law was given through Moses; grace and truth came through Jesus Christ. (John 1:16–17)

Grace and law appear to oppose one another, but this interpretation is misleading for two reasons.

The first reason is that grace and truth are divine attributes revealed to Moses immediately after the giving of the law (Exod 34:6). If the law and grace appeared together from the beginning, how could they be in conflict? It is more helpful to interpret law and grace as complementary because the giving of the law was itself act of divine grace in that the law revealed God's will for daily living. Consequently, Christ's atoning sacrifice was not God's first an act of grace.

The second reason is that grace and truth (law is a kind of prescriptive truth) go together in personal transformation. According to Calvin, because the law is concrete it is useful for educating in righteousness, for law enforcement, and for outlining how to be holy everyday (Haas 2006, 100). Everyone loves to receive grace, but not everyone likes to hear the truth because it often requires corrective action.[1]

The commentary nature of law and grace is never more obvious than in the words of Jesus:[2]

> *Do not think that I have come to abolish the Law or the Prophets; I have not come to abolish them but to fulfill them.* (Matt 5:17)

Attempts to abrogate[3] the Law of Moses in favor of grace often arise because the law divides into two parts: the holiness code and ceremonial law. This distinction arose historically because the temple in Jerusalem was destroyed by the Romans in AD 70 making it impossible to perform the ceremonial laws. However, the destruction of the temple had no such effect on the holiness code, whose prohibitions against sexual immorality were never

---

1 The existence of one set of physical laws in the universe offers interesting insight into the question of God's existence. Why is there only one set of physical laws throughout the universe? The dynamic stability of the universe points to an external, stabilizing force—God. This observation follows from Gödel's Incompleteness Theorem (Smith 2001, 89).

2 The Apostle Paul also appears to recognize the complementary nature of law and grace when he writes: "*What shall we say then? Are we to continue in sin that grace may abound? By no means! How can we who died to sin still live in it?*" (Rom 6:1–2) Grace does not excuse a libertine lifestyle, which the law helps us to avoid and remain accountable for our actions.

3 Abrogate means to repeal or do away with (a law, right, or formal agreement), usually by claiming that it no longer applies.

abolished or abrogated, as confirmed in the Council of Jerusalem in AD 50 (Acts 15:19–20).[4]

Our conduct matters. Our conduct matters to our families, for whom we model Christ and express our deepest commitments. It matters to our neighbors, for whom we witness and work for peace. It matters to God, who gave Moses the law, in whom we put our faith, and on whom we depend for our salvation. Our conduct matters.

"Honored are the pure in heart, for they shall see God." (Matt 5:8)

---

4 The holiness code is not obsolete. Consider the cleanup in New York City that occurred in the 1980s. Two criminologists, James O. Wilson and George Kelling, started the clean-up with what they called the *"broken windows"* theory. They argued: *"Crime is inevitable result of disorder. If a window is broken and left unrepaired, people walking by will conclude that no one cares and no one is in charge. Soon, more windows will be broken, and a sense of anarchy will spread from the building to the street it faces, sending the signal that anything goes. The idea is that crime is contagious."* So New York City waged a war on broken windows and graffiti in the neighborhoods and subway. Minor infractions of law were not tolerated. And crime throughout the city began to fall precipitously to everyone's surprise (White, 2004, 158). For those of us who grew up afraid to walk the streets of New York City, this outcome was shocking and radically changed the city's image.

The broken windows theory is to cities what the holiness code is to individuals. King Solomon famously wrote of the "little" sins: *"Catch the foxes for us, the little foxes that spoil the vineyards, for our vineyards are in blossom."* (Song 2:15) The point is that little things matter—they form and reflect your attitude.

❁

Eternal God,

We praise you for the beauty of the earth, the freshness of the wind, the crispness of the sea, and the warmth of dry earth. You have created heaven and earth for your glory and our benefit— thank you.

We confess that too often we say one thing and do another. Save us from our own hypocrisy.

We confess that too often we have overlooked the needs of our neighbors and preached about their shortcomings. Convert our hearts to your truth that we might display your grace.

We confess that too often we have acted too quickly out of prejudice and veiled your mercy. Grant us gracious hearts and open minds. We confess that too often we have focused on ourselves and sheltered ourselves from others. Teach us hospitality.

We confess that too often we have resisted change out of stubbornness and neglected the needs of our own youth. Give us eyes that see and ears that listen.

We confess that too often we have judged too quickly and judge imprudently. Grant us the mind of Christ.

Forgive us our many sins. Guide us in making recompense. Heal the wounds that separate us from one another and restore us to your kingdom. Through the power of the Holy Spirit and in Jesus' previous name, Amen.

Questions
1. What are six complaints among non-Christians about Christians? Which do you consider valid? How do they relate to holiness?
2. Is grace a human or a divine attribute?
3. How do truth and grace relate? Can they be separated?
4. Does God seek transformation?
5. What are two kinds of law and which one is most important?
6. What is the broken glass theory and why do I care?
7. What is the role of personal sacrifice in our testimony?

PART C: TENSION WITH OTHERS

7. HONORED ARE THE PEACEMAKERS

8. HONORED ARE THE PERSECUTED

9. HONORED ARE THE REVILED

In the final three Beatitudes, we move to tension with other people. Jesus admonishes us to share God's peace, to offer shalom to those around us, and to expect persecution and revulsion. And Jesus asks us to love our enemies and to treat hostility as an opportunity to transform lives.

We are to disciple one another, as the Apostle Paul admonishes:

> Now if anyone builds on the foundation with gold, silver, precious stones, wood, hay, straw—each one's work will become manifest, for the Day will disclose it, because it will be revealed by fire, and the fire will test what sort of work each one has done. (1 Cor 3:12–13)

The refiner's fire (Zec 13:9; Mal 3:2) points, of course, to the refiner himself whose instructions we emulate wherever life's journey takes us.

Writing about the outward journey, Nouwen (1975) sees our relationships with others moving from hostility to hospitality. Hostility comes naturally, but hospitality is more aspirational, requiring us to provide a safe place for others to become friends,[1] as the Apostle Paul writes:

> To the weak I became weak, that I might win the weak. I have become all things to all people, that by all means I might save some. (1 Cor 9:22)

---

1 (e.g. Luke 7:36–50).

Taking a risk on people's response, in the Seventh Beatitude Jesus asks us to model our lives after God and offer shalom, to become peacemakers in a world that knows no peace.

7. HONORED ARE THE PEACEMAKERS

7.1: Make Peace—Embody Shalom

7.2: Prince of Peace

7.3: Trinity of Peace

7.4: Peace on God's Terms

7.1: Make Peace—Embody Shalom

Honored are the peacemakers, for they shall be called sons of God. (Matt 5:9)

*T*he Garden of Eden begins as a picture of God's shalom whose harmony was shattered when Satan tempted Adam and Eve to eat from the tree of the knowledge of good and evil. When Adam and Eve responded by eating from the tree, they displayed more trust in Satan than in God. This broken trust shattered their intimate relationship with God and God cursed Satan saying:

> *I will put enmity between you and the woman, and between your offspring and her offspring; he shall bruise your head, and you shall bruise his heel.* (Gen 3:15)[1]

God then expelled Adam and Eve from the Garden of Eden (Gen 3:24). Adam and Eve's sin in Eden thus originated our tension with God.

The need for peacemaking followed in the first post-Eden generation, when we read:

> *So Cain was very angry, and his face fell. The LORD said to Cain, Why are you angry, and why has your face fallen? If you do well, will you not be accepted? And if you do not do well, sin is crouch-*

---

1 The second half of this verse anticipates the ministry of Christ who contends with Satan and, in his atonement, defeats sin offering us peace with God making Christ the ultimate peacemaker.

ing at the door. Its desire is for you, but you must rule over it. (Gen 4:5–7)

God saw Cain angry at his brother, Abel, and counseled Cain to avoid sin by controlling his anger (Gen 4:6–7). Unable to control his anger, Cain ignored God's counsel and murdered Abel, displaying tension within himself, with God and with his brother.[2]

In the story of Cain and Abel, God models peacemaking, a divine attribute,[3] by advising self-control, avoiding sin, and helping others. In doing so, God embodies shalom.[4] Shalom (שָׁלוֹם) means *"completeness, soundness, welfare, peace"*.[5] The Greek word for shalom (εἰρήνη; *"irene"*) has a similar scope, but more often it focuses on *"concord, peace, harmony"*.[6] The English word, *"peace"*, is almost exclusively focused on the absence of war and requires extension to encompass shalom,[7] which mitigates all three dimensions of tension.

---

2 Jesus recounts this story in the Sermon on the Mount where he links anger with murder (Matt 5:21–26).

3 *"Peacemaker"* is a also messianic title (Isaiah 9:6–7).

4 I am not the first to notice these three dimensions of peacemaking and their relationship with shalom: *"Peacemaking, therefore, is much more than a passive suffering to maintain peace or even 'bridge-building' or reconciling alienated parties. It is a demonstration of God's love through Christ in all its profundity (John 3:16, Rom 5:1 and 6–11). The peacemakers of 5:9 refers to those who, experiencing the shalom of God, become his agents establishing his peace in the world (Schniewind, Matthaus 48)."* Guelich (1982, 92).

5 (BDB 10002).

6 (BDAG 2285).

7 For example, we might talk about inner peace or peace and well-being, but peace itself is too narrow to compare with shalom.

Peacemaking is a major motif in the Sermon on the Mount. Peacemaking anticipates the next two Beatitudes and provides a context for later teaching on love, where Jesus commands:

> But I say to you, Love your enemies and pray for those who persecute you, so that you may be sons of your Father who is in heaven. For he makes his sun rise on the evil and on the good, and sends rain on the just and on the unjust. For if you love those who love you, what reward do you have? Do not even the tax collectors do the same? And if you greet only your brothers, what more are you doing than others? Do not even the Gentiles do the same? You therefore must be perfect, as your heavenly Father is perfect. (Matt 5:44–48)

Note the parallel here between *loving your enemy* and peacemaking and that God models both activities. Other applications of shalom appear in Jesus' teaching, as found in Matthew 10:

> 1. And if the house is worthy, let your peace come upon it, but if it is not worthy, let your peace return to you. (Matt 10:13)

> 2. Do not think that I have come to bring peace to the earth. I have not come to bring peace, but a sword. (Matt 10:34)

In Hebrew, *"shalom"* is used to say both hello and goodbye, but the idea of taking it with you suggests something more like hospitality. Divine hospitality, the idea of peace on earth, suggests a more political interpretation—peace as a the absence of conflict among nations—where peacemaking can be positive or negative depending on its object.[8] In first century Israel, for example, Pax Romana (translated as Roman peace) promised tranquility but delivered via a brutal occupation, not what we normally associate with peace.

The context of peacemaking is important in understanding the transformational potential of tension. For example, listen for the tension in Jesus' words to the disciples:

> *Peace I leave with you; my peace I give to you. Not as the world gives do I give to you. Let not your hearts be troubled, neither let them be afraid.* (John 14:27)

Jesus comforted to his disciples following his crucifixion in the midst of fear and uncertainty by offering them shalom. But, he went even further. In Christ's atoning death on the cross, he defeated sin and offered us peace with God.

Make peace—embody shalom.

Compassionate Father,

I give thanks for the walks that we have shared through summer

---

8 What is the object of the peace: justice, wholeness, or maintenance of privilege? (Neyrey 1998, 184)

days of my youth: the forest trails that we journeyed together; the mountain peaks that you showed me; the sandy beaches that went on and on. You held my hand, but let me lead and comforted me throughout—I worried only about the getting too much sun or avoiding the rain or just how best to have fun—Thank you. As the years went by, you never left me. Thank you. Teach me now how to take walks again in the autumn of my days: to travel paths yet untraveled with young hands eager for the journey; to offer peace and security and comfort and hospitality at odds with my nature but not with yours. Be ever near through the power of your Holy Spirit and in Jesus' name, Amen.

Questions
1. Where does disharmony (absence of peace) begin?
2. Who was the first peacemaker in the Bible?
3. What was Cain's problem? What were the components of divine peacemaking?
4. Define shalom. How does it compare to the Greek and English translations? How is shalom transformative?
5. How can Jesus command us to love one another?
6. Why is Christ's atoning sacrifice on the cross an act of peacemaking?

7.2: Prince of Peace

For *to us a child is born, to us a son is given; and the government shall be upon his shoulder, and his name shall be called Wonderful Counselor, Mighty God, Everlasting Father, Prince of Peace.* (Isa 9:6)

Shalom (שָׁלוֹם) as *"completeness, soundness, welfare, peace"*[1] is a divine attribute mostly out of reach in the Books of the Law, where brotherly conflict, not brotherly love, was the norm.

In the Books of the Law, conflict between Cain and Abel over proper worship was followed by conflict between Jacob and Esau over the birthright and inheritance (Gen 25:26–34). Later, conflict between Joseph and his brothers over their father's favoritism became so intense that Joseph's brothers sold him into slavery (Gen 37:2–28). This brotherly conflict highlights the absence of shalom and the need for divine intervention.[2]

This need for divine intervention appears even in the story of a young Moses, who attempted without success to reconcile two of his Hebrew "brothers":

> One day, when Moses had grown up, he went out to his people and looked on their burdens, and he saw an Egyptian beating a Hebrew, one of his people. He looked this way and that, and seeing no one, he struck down the Egyptian and hid him in

1 (BDB 10002).

2 In the ancient world, sibling conflict was considered an extreme form of treachery, much like spousal conflict would be perceived today (Hellerman 2001, 39–40).

the sand. When he went out the next day, behold, two Hebrews were struggling together. And he said to the man in the wrong, Why do you strike your companion? He answered, Who made you a prince and a judge over us? Do you mean to kill me as you killed the Egyptian? Then Moses was afraid, and thought, Surely the thing is known. When Pharaoh heard of it, he sought to kill Moses. But Moses fled from Pharaoh and stayed in the land of Midian. (Exod 2:11–15)

Much like God attempted to reconcile Cain and Abel, Moses attempted to reconcile two of his Hebrew brothers, but his effort fails because his own sin—murder—got in the way.

In the Books of the Prophets, peace remains out of reach as two dominant types of conflict emerge.

The first type of conflict arose between the nation of Israel and God because they repeatedly disobeyed the Mosaic covenant[3], as anticipated in Deuteronomy:

And when all these things come upon you, the blessing and the curse, which I have set before you, and you call them to mind among all the nations where the Lord your God has driven you, and return to the Lord your God, you and your children, and obey his voice in all that I command you today, with all your heart and with all your soul, then the Lord your God will restore your fortunes and have mercy on you, and he will gather you again from all the peoples where the Lord your God has scattered you. (Deut 30:1–3)

---

3 The covenant is summarized in the Ten Commandments in Exodus 20 and reiterated in Deuteronomy 5.

If the nation of Israel obeyed the covenant (practiced holiness), God promised to forgive and reunite them; however, if they ignored the covenant, God would destroy the nation and scatter the people. To remind the people of their covenantal obligations, God repeatedly sent prophets, such as Jeremiah, to warn them of their sins:

> *Their houses shall be turned over to others, their fields and wives together, for I will stretch out my hand against the inhabitants of the land, declares the LORD. For from the least to the greatest of them, everyone is greedy for unjust gain; and from prophet to priest, everyone deals falsely. They have healed the wound of my people lightly, saying, Peace, peace, when there is no peace.* (Jer 6:12–14)

Here, greedy prophets and priests, who turn their backs on sin, lead the nation to conflict with God and judgment.[4]

The second type of conflict was internal to the nation of Israel, where kings more often than not behaved badly and wandered from faith in God.

For example, when King Rehoboam, the son of Solomon, was crowned king, he was asked to reduce the heavy tax burden imposed by his father. His father's advisers counseled him to

---

4 In our own times, Bonhoeffer wrote about the problem of cheap grace—false forgiveness for false confession, saying: *"Cheap grace means grace as a doctrine, a principle, a system. It means forgiveness of sins proclaimed as a general truth, the love of God taught as the Christian 'conception' of God." "Costly grace"* requires personal confession of sin and real discipleship (Bonhoeffer 1995, 43–45).

lower taxes, but his friends counseled even higher taxes. When he raised taxes, ten tribes rebelled,[5] leaving Rehoboam only the two southern tribes, Judah and Benjamin. The other ten tribes formed a new kingdom (Israel), who crowned Jeroboam king of Israel. Jeroboam, who feared that people visiting Jerusalem for religious worship would eventually return to Rehoboam, set up alternative worship sites and recast new golden calf idols (1 Kgs 12), actions later referred to as the *"sins of Jeroboam"* (e.g. 1 Kgs 14:16).[6] Weakened by this split, both kingdoms were later destroyed and the people were exiled.

In the story of the split of the kingdom of Israel above, notice how conflict between the two nations quickly led to idolatry (Jer 1:15–16) and, by inference, tension with God. Increased tension with our neighbor naturally leads to tension with God and even with ourselves, as we strive to have our own way.

The hope of deliverance from conflict in the Old Testament came, in part, through the emergence of messianic texts, such as Isaiah 9:6–7, that link the Messiah and heaven to the idea of shalom: *"Wonderful Counselor, Mighty God, Everlasting*

5 Not only did Rehoboam divide the nation of Israel through his greedy and foolish administration (1 Kgs 12:14), he later abandoned the Law of Moses and was forced, as a consequence, to become a vassal of Shishak, the king of Egypt (2 Chr 12:1–2).

6 Animosity between the Northern and Southern kingdoms continued until New Testament times when Jews openly discriminated against Samaritans—part of the Northern Kingdom.

Father, Prince of Peace". Shalom is valuable because it is rare and because it offers a glimpse of heaven, as the Prophet Isaiah sees it:

> *The wolf shall dwell with the lamb, and the leopard*
> *shall lie down with the young goat, and the calf and*
> *the lion and the fattened calf together; and a little*
> *child shall lead them.* (Isa 11:6)

In Isaiah's vision, an end to animal predation and the picture of a little child playing without fear among dangerous animals, suggests a return to Eden and the outbreak of shalom, a sign of God's mighty work among us.

Wonderful Counselor, Mighty God, Everlasting Father, Prince of Peace,

Oh Lord, to be like you—strong and wise and patience and peace loving.

Oh, to be a covenant keeper, dependable and steady, a pillar against the wind.

Oh, to offer mercy and grace and patience and love and truth to all who come near: hospitality in the desert; peace amidst confusion; security when uncertainty tears at the soul.

Oh Lord, to be like you; to be like you.

Remember us, Lord, but forget the sin that depletes our strength, leaves us foolish, makes us impatient, and creates dissension.

Remember us, Lord, but forgive our transgressions.

Remember us, Lord, but wipe away our iniquity that leaves us judgmental and arrogant and at odds with all things good and true.

Remember us, Lord, lest we forget ourselves. In the power of your Holy Spirit grant us a new day and the strength to live it in a new way following the example of your Son and our Savior, Jesus Christ, Amen.

Questions
1. Is shalom common in the Old Testament?
2. Why is conflict in the Old Testament so frequently between brothers?
3. Was Moses a successful peacemaker?
4. What two types of conflict do we observe in the Old Testament?
5. Why is peacemaking a messianic attribute?

7.3: Trinity of Peace

On the evening of that day, the first day of the week, the doors being locked where the disciples were for fear of the Jews, Jesus came and stood among them and said to them, Peace be with you. When he had said this, he showed them his hands and his side. Then the disciples were glad when they saw the Lord. Jesus said to them again, Peace be with you. As the Father has sent me, even so I am sending you. (John 20:19–21)

When we focus solely on peace as reconciliation among feuding folks—relief of the tension with our brothers and sisters, we miss the significance of God's peace—shalom—breaking out throughout scripture. Remember that shalom (שָׁלוֹם) means *"completeness, soundness, welfare, peace"*.[1] It also implies healing, restoration, reconciliation, and salvation—not just hello and goodbye (as it is often used in Hebrew), but a return to Eden. Shalom implies inner peace, peace with God, and peace between brothers and sisters—a trinity of peace.

If this Trinitarian interpretation of peace seems far-fetched, remember that the Beatitudes and Jesus' call sermon at Nazareth (Luke 4:14–21) start with the words of the Prophet Isaiah:

> *The Spirit of the Lord GOD is upon me, because the LORD has anointed me to bring good news to the poor; he has sent me to bind up the brokenhearted, to proclaim liberty to the captives, and the opening*

---

1 (BDB 10002).

of the prison to those who are bound; to proclaim
the year of the LORD's favor, and the day of ven-
geance of our God; to comfort all who mourn; to
grant to those who mourn in Zion—to give them a
beautiful headdress instead of ashes, the oil of glad-
ness instead of mourning, the garment of praise in-
stead of a faint spirit; that they may be called oaks
of righteousness, the planting of the LORD, that he
may be glorified. (Isa 61:1–3)

Notice the inner peace referenced with the phrase: *"bind up the brokenhearted"*; notice the peace with God referenced with the phrase: *"The Spirit of the Lord GOD is upon me"*; notice the peace with brothers and sisters referenced with the phrase: *"to proclaim liberty to the captives"*. In effect, God himself has initiated a trinity of peace—inner peace, peace with God, and peace among brothers and sisters—which broke out with the coming of Christ, as Isaiah prophesied and to which we will now turn.

Inner Peace. What could bring peace more quickly than physical and mental healing, as Jesus' miracles attest? Jesus' first miracle after leaving Nazareth occurs in the synagogue in Capernaum[2] where Jesus drives out a demon out of a man (Luke 4:31–36). After that man was healed, demon deliverance ministry becomes a common occurrence (Luke 4:41).

Jesus' healing transformed a person so dramatically that it was obvious just looking at them, as we witness with the heal-

---

2 Peter's home town (Luke 4:38).

ing of the man with the unclean spirit in the Gerasenes:

> *And they came to Jesus and saw the demon-pos-*
> *sessed man, the one who had had the legion, sitting*
> *there, clothed and in his right mind, and they were*
> *afraid.* (Mark 5:15)

The healed man immediately becomes an evangelist (Mark 5:20), much like the woman at the well (John 4:28–30), because the presence of God—the shalom of God—is news that we cannot keep to ourselves.

Peace with God. Many people today take peace with God for granted, as if sin and the wrath of God were suddenly of no consequence. However, the Bible reminds us that Jerusalem was destroyed first by the Babylonians and later by the Romans for the sin of refusing, ignoring, and killing the prophets (Matt 23:34–47); events provoked by sin and God's response to it.

This problem of sin persists. In the Old Testament, prophets reminded the people of their obligations under the Mosaic covenant—in other words, their sin. In the New Testament, Jesus Christ atones for our sin with his death on the cross, as Paul writes:

> *For I delivered to you as of first importance what I*
> *also received: that Christ died for our sins in accor-*
> *dance with the Scriptures, that he was buried, that*
> *he was raised on the third day in accordance with*
> *the Scriptures, and that he appeared to Cephas*

[Peter], then to the twelve. (1 Cor 15:3–5)

Of first importance, Christ's atoning sacrifice makes peace with God possible. If we claim to have no sin (or deny its importance) and refuse to acknowledge Christ's atoning sacrifice, then our sin and guilt remain. If unrepentant sin led to the destruction of the temple and the city of Jerusalem, then why would God spare unrepentant and sinful people in Corinth or, for that matter, in Washington or New York?

Sin still matters and the unrepentant still must face judgment before a wrathful God, but:

> *God so loved the world, that he gave his only Son,*
> *that whoever believes in him should not perish but*
> *have eternal life.* (John 3:16)

God provided for our salvation through Jesus' death on the cross which brings us to peace with Him.

Peace among others. We normally think of peace in terms of reconciliation, in part, because peace on earth is so hard to obtain, as the Apostle Paul admonishes: "*If possible, so far as it depends on you, live peaceably with all.*" (Rom 12:18) Here Paul is focusing on interpersonal conflict, not the more generous shalom of Christ that we see, for example, in Jesus' first miracle where he rescues the wedding of an impoverished couple of newlyweds from social embarrassment:

Now there were six stone water jars there for the Jewish rites of purification, each holding twenty or thirty gallons. Jesus said to the servants, Fill the jars with water. And they filled them up to the brim. And he said to them, Now draw some out and take it to the master of the feast. So they took it. When the master of the feast tasted the water now become wine, and did not know where it came from (though the servants who had drawn the water knew), the master of the feast called the bridegroom and said to him, Everyone serves the good wine first, and when people have drunk freely, then the poor wine. But you have kept the good wine until now. (John 2:6–10)

Notice that Jesus' miracle has both a quantitative and a qualitative dimension. Quantitatively, we are talking about a lot of wine—six times twenty is one hundred and twenty gallons of wine. Qualitatively, the master of ceremonies (ἀρχιτρίκλινος)[3] is surprised by the wine's quality. Quantitatively and qualitatively, Jesus' generosity enabled this young couple to avoid social embarrassment and to live at peace within their community.

As in the wedding at Cana, Jesus delivers so much more peace than we expect or deserve.

---

3 Weddings were a community responsibility and minimum standards were required to assure that everyone contributed their fair share. The master of ceremonies (or steward) was hired to monitor those contributions.

❀

Great Physician, Prince of Peace, Lord of the Sabbath,

Where can we find shalom but with you? Holy Spirit grant us your peace. As our bodies are at war within us . . . We want to be filled with your peace, but impatiently fill our stomachs beyond need, imprudently pop pills for the slightest ailments, and tirelessly talk about religion without making room for you in our busy schedules. Heal our hearts, bodies, and minds; grant us your peace.

Where can we find shalom but with you? Gentle Father grant us your peace. As we neglect our fellowship with you . . . We want to be faithful worshipers, servants, and ministers, serving you but more nearly trying to get our own way unfaithfully constructing idols of things great and small, hoping in total foolishness to bribe and control you. Forgive our sin; look beyond our transgressions; pardon our iniquity.

Where can we find shalom but with you? Jesus grant us your peace. As our relationships are in tatters…We want to be faithful children, parents, and spouses; not imprudently looking to be served by those around us rather than serving or jealously demanding more from others than from ourselves. Heal our families and relationships; grant us your peace.

Grant us your abundant peace, in Jesus' precious name,
Amen.

Questions
1. Why is the concept of shalom important in interpreting the New Testament?
2. Where is Jesus' call sermon recorded and what Old Testament passage is it based on?
3. How would you explain the phrase: bind up the brokenhearted?
4. What do peacemaking and healing relate to one another?
5. Why were witnesses to the healing the man with the unclean spirit in the Gerasenes afraid? How did they know he had been healed?
6. What does the Apostle Paul view as of *first importance* in 1 Corinthians 15:3? Why?
7. Why is the destruction of Jerusalem in AD 70 important to us today? Do we need peace with God?

7.4: Peace on God's Terms

But the fruit of the Spirit is love, joy, peace, patience, kindness, goodness, faithfulness, gentleness, self-control; against such things there is no law. (Gal 5:22–23)

*R*eceive shalom, extend shalom. Shalom starts with God; works in our hearts; and then is extended to others, just like other fruits of the Spirit (Gal 5:22–23). And just as the apple does not fall far from the tree, as we find our identity in Christ, his example plays out in our lives. *"Honored are the peacemakers, for they shall be called children of God."* (Matt 5:9)[1]

Even for obedient children, moving from theory into practice is hard. Instead of peacemaking, we prefer a selfish form of peace—peace on our terms. Pax Romana was peace on Rome's terms; Pax America is peace on Washington's terms; shalom is peace on God's terms. As a fruit of the Spirit, shalom is the one fruit of the spirit that needs to be enjoyed together with all the others, as the Apostle Paul observes:

> *Now the works of the flesh are evident: sexual immorality, impurity, sensuality, idolatry, sorcery, enmity, strife, jealousy, fits of anger, rivalries, dissensions, divisions, envy, drunkenness, orgies, and things like these. I warn you, as I warned you before, that those who do such things will not inherit*

---

1 The ancient church was modeled after patrilineal family group which implies that we all brothers and sisters with one, eternal father (Matt 23:9). It is interesting to see Jesus himself allude to this family model (Hellerman 2001).

the kingdom of God. But the fruit of the Spirit is love, joy, peace, patience, kindness, goodness, faithfulness, gentleness, self-control; against such things there is no law. And those who belong to Christ Jesus have crucified the flesh with its passions and desires. (Gal 5:19–24)

To move from fleshly passion to inner peace, two movements are necessary: throwing off sin (becoming holy) and taking on godliness (imitating God), both through the Holy Spirit. Through confession of sin, (through the Holy Spirit) we move to throw off sin; through modeling ourselves on Christ, (through the Holy Spirit) we move to take on his righteousness. Both movements bring peace into our relationships in the family, community, church, work, and the world (Graham 1955, 92–95).

The peace of Christ, expressed in the Seventh Beatitude, moved me on August 4, 1972 to write the following to my draft board:

I cannot fight in a war because as a Christian my highest duty is to follow the teachings of Jesus Christ. I believe that life is the sacred gift of God which is to be honored and respected by all men. I believe that every man has a constructive contribution to make to humanity and that each man has the right to fulfill this destiny. I believe there is a beauty in all life and that we should use love, concern, and non-violent methods to solve our conflicts. I believe all men are of one indivisible whole and that each man's life is important to the life of the whole. I must live in peace to uphold my faith.

On New Year's Eve of that year, a peace agreement was signed, America's involvement in the Vietnam War ended, and my draft number (13) was never called. Called or not, my life changed forever—my opposition to the war spilled into my family life and influenced later career decisions.[2]

Decisions about the Vietnam War divided many families in the 1960s and 1970s, but opposition to the war did not lead to a lasting peace. Peace on God's terms requires more than peace treaties and changes in governments.[3] As Christians, we must seek peace within ourselves, with God, and with others on a daily basis. World peace may not be within our grasp, but like the Good Samaritan (Luke 10:25–37) we can, at least, express the love of Christ to the needy person who crosses our path.[4]

Jesus said: *"Honored are the peacemakers, for they shall be called sons and daughters of God."* (Matt 5:9)

---

2 Neyrey (1998, 184) notes that it is this family context where Jesus says: *"Do not think that I have come to bring peace to the earth. I have not come to bring peace, but a sword."* (Matt 10:34)

3 Mouw (2010, 65) sees moral simplicity accompanied by openness to God's grace as a path towards sanctification and cites the examples of Corrie ten Boom and Mother Teresa.

4 Why is the Good Samaritan not called the Great Samaritan? He did what was necessary, not everything possible, to save a man's life (Cloud and Townsend 1992, 38–39).

Holy and Gracious God,

In the power of your Holy Spirit, help us to separate ourselves from sexual immorality, impurities, sensuality, idolatry, and sorcery, fleeing from enmity, strife, jealousy, fits of anger, dissensions, divisions, and envy, refusing to engage in drunkenness and orgies. Through the example of Jesus Christ, bid us to pursue the fruits of the spirit by practicing love, joy, peace, patience, kindness, goodness, faithfulness, gentleness, and self-control (Gal 5:19–24). Crucify the passions of the flesh that naturally grow in us. May peace on your terms grow to become our peace on our terms and may we share it with those around us. In Jesus' precious name, Amen.

Questions
1. How does peacemaking point to God?
2. What is Pax Romana? Why does it pose a cautionary tale for us?
3. How would you characterize the righteousness of Christ?
4. What are the lessons of Vietnam?
5. What is the lesson of the Good Samaritan?

8. HONORED ARE THE PERSECUTED

8.1: Promote Righteousness

8.2: Righteous Suffering

8.3: Christian Paradox

8.4: Bless Those that Persecute

8.1: *Promote Righteousness*

Honored are those who are persecuted for righteousness' sake, for theirs is the kingdom of heaven. (Matt 5:10)

For many Christians, persecution poses a perplexing question—*"Why are good people persecuted?"* (Graham 1955, 98)—to which the Book of James responds:

> *Count it all joy, my brothers, when you meet trials of various kinds, for you know that the testing of your faith produces steadfastness. And let steadfastness have its full effect, that you may be perfect and complete, lacking in nothing.* (Jas 1:2–4)

The paradox of the suffering servant at the heart of the Christian worldview was first expressed by the Prophet Isaiah:

> *Out of the anguish of his soul he shall see and be satisfied; by his knowledge shall the righteous one, my servant, make many to be accounted righteous, and he shall bear their iniquities.* (Isa 53:11)

In effect, what James is saying is that persecution for righteousness' sake both shapes us in sanctification and marks us as disciples of Christ, who was himself persecuted unto death.

Here the word, persecution (διώκω; *"dioko"*), means: *"to harass someone, esp. because of beliefs, persecute"*[1] and it often associated in the Old Testament with a military engagement vigorously pursued (e.g. Deut 11:4).[2] The word, *"righteousness"*

1 (BDAG 2059(2)).
2 Guelich (1982, 93) notes that the perfect participle form of the word

(δικαιοσύνη; *"dikiosune"*), means: *"the quality or characteristic of upright behavior, uprightness, righteousness"*.[3] As we hunger and thirst for righteousness, we expect others to persecute us, as scripture reminds us (1 Pet 4:16).[4]

The injustice of Jesus' persecution is noted by one of the other men being crucified,[5] as Luke's Gospel records:

> *One of the criminals who were hanged railed at him, saying, Are you not the Christ? Save yourself and us! But the other rebuked him, saying, Do you not fear God, since you are under the same sentence of condemnation? And we indeed justly, for we are receiving the due reward of our deeds; but this man has done nothing wrong. And he said, Jesus, remember me when you come into your kingdom. And he said to him, Truly, I say to you, today you will be with me in Paradise.* (Luke 23:39–43)

Note that this story mentions both the idea of righteous persecution and the reward of heaven, as cited in the Eighth Beatitude.

Persecution (unto death) in the Old Testament begins with the story of Cain and Abel, where Cain kills Abel because God accepted Abel's righteous sacrifice and rejected his own (Gen 4:3–9). Post-resurrection persecution in the New Testament begins with the stoning of Stephen who accused the Sanhedrin of

(δεδιωγμένοι) is uniquely used here and it suggests an actual community experience, not a hypothetical possibility.

3 (BDAG 2004 (3)).

4 *"Yet if anyone suffers as a Christian, let him not be ashamed, but let him glorify God in that name."* (1 Pet 4:16)

5 This association of persecution with righteousness is also found in Isaiah 53.

false worship, persecution of the prophets, and murdering God's Messiah (Acts 7:48–53). Persecution is likely also to be our fate, as the Apostle Paul reminds us:

> *Who shall separate us from the love of Christ? Shall tribulation, or distress, or persecution, or famine, or nakedness, or danger, or sword? As it is written, For your sake we are being killed all the day long; we are regarded as sheep to be slaughtered. No, in all these things we are more than conquerors through him who loved us.* (Rom 8:35–37)

Persecution is often edited out of this passage in public readings, but it is fundamental to our life in Christ.

Jesus reminds us that a student is not better than his teacher—he was persecuted; we will be persecuted (Matt 10:24–25). But even in the midst of persecution, Jesus admonishes us to—*"Love your enemies and pray for those who persecute you"* (Matt 5:44)—suggesting that persecution is an ministry opportunity.

Almighty Father,

We give thanks for the many blessings that you have given us. Among these gifts are your presence, your name, your covenantal grace, and our salvation in Jesus Christ. May we continue to be blessed and bless others (Gen 12:1–3). Sanctify us in your righteousness that we might be fit stewards of your grace. And if our sanctification includes persecution, grant us the strength to bear it with dignity and grace. And may we ever remain in your love May we share it with others until we meet you again in glory. In Jesus' name, Amen.

Questions
1. What is the fruit of the testing of our faith, according to the Book of James?
2. What comment did the criminal being crucified with Jesus make about his guilt?
3. What was the first story of religious persecution in the Bible?
4. Why was Stephen martyred?
5. What does Jesus say about teachers and students in Matthew 10?

8.2: Righteous Suffering

Then the LORD said, I have surely seen the affliction of my people who are in Egypt and have heard their cry because of their task-masters. I know their sufferings (Exod 3:7).

*I*n the Books of the Law and the Prophets, the Jewish experience of God frequently arises in the context of suffering.

In the Books of the Law, Moses suffered living as a refugee in the desert and shepherding his father-in-law's sheep far from his home and family in Egypt. Exiled from Egypt, shamed by his own inept leadership, and fearful of legal prosecution for murder, Moses found himself before a burning bush in the presence of God (Exod 3:1),[1] who called him for a new assignment:

> Come, I will send you to Pharaoh that you may bring my people, the children of Israel, out of Egypt. (Exod 3:10)

Egypt is in his heart and on his mind, but Moses does not jump at the idea of returning to Egypt because, having murdered an Egyptian, returning entailed obvious personal risk. Mitigating the risks are three important assurances that God gives to Moses which take the forms of His presence, His name, and His covenant (the Law).

Presence. The assurance of God's presence is a blessing in

---

1 What do you see when you look into a fire? Some people see a natural Rorschach test. Was Moses' own soul a burning bush?

the form of comfort, provision, and protection—things Moses lacked when he attempted to lead his people without God's help. In revealing his presence to Moses, the uncertainty of the mission in Egypt is immediately reduced (Rom 8:31) and its success is assured: *"But I will be with you"* (Exod 3:12). God's presence is further secured when God reveals his name, and, later, offers a covenant to Moses.

The Name. The assurance of knowing God's name was no small deal in the ancient world. The ancients believed that knowing the name of a god gave one power over that god. When God gave Moses his name, he was, at a minimum, offering him a direct line of communication—personal prayer—with God.

The meaning of God's covenant name was also significant—YHWH which in Hebrew means *"I will be who I will be"* or *"I am who I am" (Exod 3:14–15)*—and new: A REAL GOD (one that really exists) with REAL POWER (sovereign everywhere, not just a local, neighborhood god). Local gods were the norm in the ancient world, in part, because leaders wanted to lay claim to their territories and to seek their intervention (typically through sacrifices) in the spiritual world.[2] God's interventions on behalf of Moses were not unusual from an ancient perspective, but what

---

2 Biblical echoes of this line of thinking are found in (Judg 11:30–40; 1 Kgs 12:26–29)

was unusual was that God traveled with Moses out of Egypt and into the Promised Land.

The Covenant (Law). The covenant helped secure Moses' experience of God presence because in the covenant God revealed his will to the people of Israel, something uncommon in the ancient world—prayer is really difficult when one neither knows a god's name nor what that god desires. God revealed to Moses that He was both a covenant maker and covenant keeper.

The covenant of Moses begins with a preamble: *"I am the LORD your God, who brought you out of the land of Egypt, out of the house of slavery."* (Exod 20:2). The preamble makes clear that God cares about the people of Israel enough to intervene on their behalf and the Law instructs them on how to live in peace and righteousness, making God's presence concrete in daily life.

In the Books of the Prophets, no one suffers more than Job even though he is a righteous man:

> *There was a man in the land of Uz whose name was Job, and that man was blameless and upright, one who feared God and turned away from evil.* (Job 1:1)

Job is so righteous that even God brags about him to Satan:

> *Have you considered my servant Job, that there is none like him on the earth, a blameless and upright man, who fears God and turns away from*

evil? (Job 1:8)

To which Satan asks God's permission to test him and God grants permission for Satan to take everything Job has away and to afflict him with horrible suffering (Job 1–2). In righteous suffering, Job feels a need to seek out and to rely on God, rather than his own resources, and, in his misery, to seek a savior:[3] *"For I know that my Redeemer lives, and at the last he will stand upon the earth."* (Job 19:25)[4]

This redemption theme, of relying solely on God, is repeated in the story of Daniel's friends, Shadrach, Meshach, and Abednego. When Daniel's friends refuse to worship King Nebuchadnezzar's golden idol instead of the one true God, they are thrown into the fiery furnace, as we read:

> *And these three men, Shadrach, Meshach, and Abednego, fell bound into the burning fiery furnace. Then King Nebuchadnezzar was astonished*

---

3 The Prophet Jeremiah writes: *"Behold, the days are coming, declares the LORD, when I will make a new covenant with the house of Israel and the house of Judah, not like the covenant that I made with their fathers on the day when I took them by the hand to bring them out of the land of Egypt, my covenant that they broke, though I was their husband, declares the LORD. For this is the covenant that I will make with the house of Israel after those days, declares the LORD: I will put my law within them, and I will write it on their hearts. And I will be their God, and they shall be my people. And no longer shall each one teach his neighbor and each his brother, saying, 'Know the LORD,' for they shall all know me, from the least of them to the greatest, declares the LORD. For I will forgive their iniquity, and I will remember their sin no more."* (Jer 31:31–34)

4 Some believe that Moses used the story of Job's righteous suffering to convince the people of Israel to leave slavery in Egypt, which would make the Book of Job the oldest book in the Bible. For example, see: Geisler (2007, 189–195).

and rose up in haste. He declared to his counselors, Did we not cast three men bound into the fire? They answered and said to the king, True, O king. He answered and said, But I see four men unbound, walking in the midst of the fire, and they are not hurt; and the appearance of the fourth is like a son of the gods. (Dan 3:23–25)

Righteous suffering not only leads us to rely on God, it gives testimony to God's glory.

Righteous suffering is paradoxically honored in the Eighth Beatitude: *"Honored are those who are persecuted for righteousness' sake, for theirs is the kingdom of heaven."* (Matt 5:10) Jesus later ties righteous suffering to eternal life: *"Whoever finds his life will lose it, and whoever loses his life for my sake will find it."* (Matt 10:39)[5]

Eternal and Compassionate God,

We thank you, Lord, for visiting us when we are afflicted and suffer unjustly. For you are a God who cares, who understands our grief, our wounds, our sorrows, our diseases. We lay our afflictions before you for we cannot bear them alone. Heal our

---

5 This paradox appears in numerous places in the New Testament. For example, the Apostle Paul writes: *"So death is at work in us, but life in you."* (2 Cor 4:12). Also, (Jas 1:2–3) and (1 Pet 4:12).

wounds, comfort us in our griefs, and purge us of disease. Restore us; redeem us; save us; in doing so teach us to bear the wounds, griefs, and diseases of those around us and to point them to you. Teach us to intercede for the people around us in action and in prayer. For you are our God and we are your people. You are with us; you are for us; and you have given your name to us. In the power of your Holy Spirit, let our security reside only in you, now and always. In Jesus' name, Amen.

Questions

1. Why do you think that we frequently encounter God in the midst of suffering?
2. What are three resources that God provides Moses in his returning to Egypt?
3. What is special about God telling Moses his name? What about divine presence?
4. What is the significance of God providing Moses the law?
5. What are two reasons that Job's suffering differs from most of ours?
6. What is special about righteous suffering?
7. What is the Christian paradox?

8.3: *Christian Paradox*

He himself bore our sins in his body on the tree, that we might die to sin and live to righteousness. By his wounds you have been healed. (1 Pet 2:24)

*J*esus teaches us to practice humility while pursuing righteousness even if we suffer shame, persecution, and death, as he did on the cross. Because death is the penalty for sin (Gen 3:3), Jesus' righteous death on the cross allowed him to pay the penalty of our sin (1 Pet 2:24; 1 Cor 15:3) and his resurrection identified him as the son of God.[1] This linking of sin to the penalty of death is critical to understanding Christ's atoning work on the cross.

Christ's atoning death runs against our usual assumption that our debt for sin is, not against God, but against our neighbor. For example, discrimination, a form of persecution against our neighbor, results in tensions over racial, ethnic, class, and gender equality, as the Apostle Paul taught:

> *For as many of you as were baptized into Christ have put on Christ. There is neither Jew nor Greek [racial and ethnic equality], there is neither slave nor free [economic equality], there is no male and female [gender equality], for you are all one in*

---

1 Jesus referred to himself as the Son of Man. Out of 189 verses in the Bible that use this term, 89 are found in Ezekiel,   which refer to the prophet himself. The term in Hebrew literally means *"son of Adam"* (Ezek 2:1). In the more famous passage in Dan 7:13, the Hebrew expression is the more familiar *"son of man"*.

Christ Jesus. (Gal 3:27–28)

Being one in Christ means that we model our lives after both Christ's humble life and death so that humility replaces pride, discrimination, and persecution in our own lives, as evidenced in our treatment of others.

Modeling humility, Jesus offers many alternatives to violence in dealing with persecution, including:

> *1. Do not resist the one who is evil. But if anyone slaps you on the right cheek, turn to him the other also* (Matt 5:39)
>
> *2. Love your enemies and pray for those who persecute you* (Matt 5:44).
>
> *3. And if anyone forces you to go one mile, go with him two miles.* (Matt 5:41)
>
> *4. Judge not, that you be not judged.* (Matt 7:1)
>
> *5. ...render to Caesar the things that are Caesar's, and to God the things that are God's.* (Matt 22:21)

Refusing to defend oneself (one's honor) could lead to perilous outcomes in a first century legal context because one was expected to offer one's own defense, but it is absolutely necessary if persecution is to become a ministry opportunity, as we are told:

> *But before all this they will lay their hands on you and persecute you, delivering you up to the synagogues and prisons, and you will be brought before kings and governors for my name's sake. This will be your opportunity to bear witness.* (Luke 21:12–

13)

We see this principle illustrated firsthand when Stephen refused to offer his own defense before the Sanhedrin and chose instead to defend Christ (Acts 7).

Stephen was the first among many Christian martyrs,[2] but other early Christians risked their lives in living testimony through service, as during a plague in Alexandria in the third century Christians refused to abandon the city and remained to care for the sick.[3] A recent example of such fearless service was seen among Christian doctors working during the Ebola outbreak in West Africa.

A life of fearless service is possible because in Christ's resurrection life follows death—the origin of Christian paradox.

Loving Father,

We give thanks for the life and death of Jesus who lived a humble life and bore our sins on the cross. Help us to practice humble-

2 The only apostle that was not martyred was the Apostle John (Foxe 2001, 10) Martyrdom was so common that in the Book of Revelation appears to endorse the idea of two resurrections in the end times—one is for the martyrs who rule with Christ for a thousand years, and the other is other Christians (Rev 20:5).

3 Kinnaman and Lyons (2007, 110) ask this question noting that the absence of empathy among Christians during the AIDS epidemic has been a major source of the antipathy among gays towards the church.

ness and hospitality with all people. Help us to put on Christ's righteousness and defend your honor, not ours. Help us to pay our bills and our taxes, to turn the other cheek, to treat our enemies with love and respect, and to judge the actions, not the intensions, of those around us. In all we do, help us to practice racial, ethnic, class, and gender equality. In the power of your Holy Spirit, may conflict and bickering and gossip end with us. In Jesus' name, Amen.

Questions
1. What forms of equality does the Apostle Paul address in Galatians 3:27–28?
2. What does sin have to do with Christ's atoning death on the cross?
3. Why does Jesus' teaching on persecution spur discussion? Which teaching strikes you as most controversial?
4. What does Jesus teach about dealing with honor challenges?
5. Were there more martyrs to the faith in the first century than today? Why or why not?
6. What is special historically about the Christian response to epidemics?

8.4: Bless Those that Persecute

Bless *those who persecute you; bless and do not curse them.* (Rom 12:14)

*I*ncreasingly even in America, Christians find themselves the target of isolation, discrimination, persecution, and shootings. Few will forget the shooting of young, female, high school student in 1999 for professing faith in Jesus Christ, yet it happened again in 2015.[1] During 2015 alone, a woman was jailed for publically espousing Biblical views on marriage;[2] a church was the site of a mass shooting;[3] and Christians were publicly beheaded by Islamic extremists. From the cross, *"Jesus said, Father, forgive them, for they know not what they do."* (Luke 23:34) Like the crucifixion, persecution reminds us of who we are, who we belong to, and what we are about.

Who We Are. Persecution links our identity to Christ, as Jesus reminds us: *"Rejoice and be glad, for your reward is great in heaven, for so they persecuted the prophets who were before you."* (Matt 5:12) Persecution for righteousness sake validates our faith and places us in the company of prophets.

Who We Belong To. Like the prophets, we are citizens of heaven (Phil 3:20) and undocumented aliens here on earth, as

1 http://www.CassiereneBernall.org. Also: (Saslow, Kaplan, and Hoyt, 2015).
2 (Ellis and Payne 2015).
3 (Wikipedia 2015a)

the Apostle Peter writes:

> *Once you were not a people, but now you are God's people; once you had not received mercy, but now you have received mercy. Beloved, I urge you as sojourners and exiles to abstain from the passions of the flesh, which wage war against your soul. Keep your conduct among the Gentiles honorable, so that when they speak against you as evildoers, they may see your good deeds and glorify God on the day of visitation.* (1 Pet 2:10–12)

Honorable conduct and good deeds mark us as Christians so as the body of Christ people should see something different about us, especially in persecution.[4]

What We Are About. Persecution is part of the mix of trials that we should expect to experience,[5] as the Apostle Peter writes:

> *Now who is there to harm you if you are zealous for what is good? But even if you should suffer for righteousness' sake, you will be blessed. Have no*

---

4 *"Listen to me, you who pursue righteousness, you who seek the LORD: look to the rock from which you were hewn, and to the quarry from which you were dug."* (Isa 51:1)

5 *"Who is to condemn? Christ Jesus is the one who died—more than that, who was raised—who is at the right hand of God, who indeed is interceding for us. Who shall separate us from the love of Christ? Shall tribulation, or distress, or persecution, or famine, or nakedness, or danger, or sword? As it is written, For your sake we are being killed all the day long; we are regarded as sheep to be slaughtered. No, in all these things we are more than conquerors through him who loved us. For I am sure that neither death nor life, nor angels nor rulers, nor things present nor things to come, nor powers, nor height nor depth, nor anything else in all creation, will be able to separate us from the love of God in Christ Jesus our Lord."* (Rom 8:34–39)

> *fear of them, nor be troubled, but in your hearts honor Christ the Lord as holy, always being prepared to make a defense to anyone who asks you for a reason for the hope that is in you; yet do it with gentleness and respect, having a good conscience, so that, when you are slandered, those who revile your good behavior in Christ may be put to shame. For it is better to suffer for doing good, if that should be God's will, than for doing evil.* (1 Pet 3:13–17)

Are we zealous for what is good? Do we suffer for righteousness sake? Persecution trains us to lean on Christ—the source of our goodness and righteousness— and not our own abilities, prejudices, and strength.

When Jesus teaches us about being salt, it is attached to a warning:

> *You are the salt of the earth, but if salt has lost its taste, how shall its saltiness be restored? It is no longer good for anything except to be thrown out and trampled under people's feet.* (Matt 5:13)

If we lose touch with Christ, we are like an unplugged vacuum cleaner showing potential, but no power—trampling is a good analogy for the persecution of a church that has lost its way.[6]

It's better to be persecuted for righteousness sake, *"so*

---

6 For example, total membership in the Presbyterian Church (USA) has declined from 3,100,951 in 1984 to 1,667,767 in 2014 (Wikipedia 2015c). This is a loss of about half (46%) in 30 years or an average of 1.5 % per year. Meanwhile, total U.S. population has grown from 225 million in 1980 to 309 million in 2010 or 36 percent or about 1.2 percent per year (Wikipedia 2015b). In other words, membership has fallen even as population has increased.

that, when you are slandered, those who revile your good behavior in Christ may be put to shame" (1 Pet 3:16–17), as Jesus reminds us in the Eighth Beatitude: *"Bless those who persecute you; bless and do not curse them."* (Rom 12:14)

God of All Wonders,

The heavens declare your glory and we are witnesses to it. Our eyes have seen and our ears have heard of the splendor of your creation. We give testimony to the love that you showered on us when Jesus died a cruel death in our place and for our salvation he rose from the dead. How can our lips then be silent? We are citizens of heaven and sojourners in this land. Teach us, Lord, to testify in humility to your love for us; to abstain from the passions of this life that wage war on our souls; and to share your passion for our lives and salvation with gentleness and respect. If we then should suffer, then may it be for your kingdom and your righteousness and not for our own sin. In the power of your Holy Spirit, help us to be salt and light. In Jesus' precious name and for his glory. Amen.

※

Questions

1. Is persecution of Christians a problem in America?
2. What three things does persecution remind us of?
3. What warning does Jesus offer when he talks about salt?
4. According the Apostle Peter, how are we to offer a defense of the faith?
5. How does persecution help us order our priorities? What is our first priority?

9. HONORED ARE THE REVILED

9.1: Persecution Gets Personal

9.2: Suffering Often Predates Salvation

9.3: Persecution Can Be Transformative

9.4: Persecution and Lethargy

9.1: Persecution Gets Personal

Honored are you when others revile you and persecute you and utter all kinds of evil against you falsely on my account. (Matt 5:11)

*T*he Ninth Beatitude is the capstone Beatitude, which repeats Eighth Beatitude emphatically, in content, intensity, and position.[1]

Notice the verbs—revile, persecute, slander—the emphasis screams at us, the tension with others is intensified. Notice how the object of this vitriol shifts from righteousness (in general) to me (specifically), as generic persecution has become a personal attack (Wilkins 2004, 211).[2] Notice how the tension is amplified by the shift from the third person (they) to the second person (you) (Neyrey 1998, 168). Notice the intensification comes on top of the repetition of the Eight Beatitude and on top of being the capstone Beatitude—the emphasis here simply screams.

The key verb here is revile (ὀνειδίζω; *"onedizo"*) which means: *"to find fault in a way that demeans the other, reproach,*

---

1 The parallel in Luke's Gospel is even more explicit: *"Honored are you when people hate you and when they exclude you and revile you and spurn your name as evil, on account of the Son of Man!"* (Luke 6:22)

2 Guelich (1982, 94): *"The differences between Matthew and Luke reflect different settings in the Church's mission. Persecution is a more general expression for the antagonistic behavior experienced by the Church in mission, while exclusion* (ἀφορίζω), *Luke 6:22) may well refer to the earlier, more specific mission within the synagogue setting..."*

revile, mock, heap insults upon as a way of shaming"[3] and which is closely related to the noun form (ὄνειδος; *"onedos"*) of the word which means: *"loss of standing connected with disparaging speech, disgrace, reproach, insult"*.[4]

The meaning of these words was intensified by Jesus' body language. Jesus looks his disciples in the eye and addresses them as friends, like a commander knowing that when the battle begins they will have his back—this is an intense moment.[5] Yet, the commander-pep-talk analogy breaks down because the disciples ultimately do not have his back and Jesus knows that he goes alone to the cross. Nevertheless, the coming cross gives urgency and intensity to this discussion because the disciples will be left behind and they must deal with persecution and revulsion on their own, especially when it involves their closest family and friends.

Reviled is used biblically in several specific contexts:

> *1. She conceived and bore a son and said, God has taken away my reproach.* (Gen 30:23)

---

3 (BDAG 5316(1)).

4 (BDAG 5318).

5 The Apostle Paul writes: *"For while we were still weak, at the right time Christ died for the ungodly. For one will scarcely die for a righteous person—though perhaps for a good person one would dare even to die—but God shows his love for us in that while we were still sinners, Christ died for us."* (Rom 5:6–8) The fact that disciples did not stand in solidarity with Jesus when he was arrested which makes Christ's sacrifice even more poignant.

2. If a man takes his sister, a daughter of his father or a daughter of his mother, and sees her nakedness, and she sees his nakedness, it is a disgrace, and they shall be cut off in the sight of the children of their people. He has uncovered his sister's nakedness, and he shall bear his iniquity. (Lev 20:17)

3. He will swallow up death forever; and the Lord GOD will wipe away tears from all faces, and the reproach of his people he will take away from all the earth, for the LORD has spoken. (Isa 25:8)

4. But I am a worm and not a man, scorned by mankind and despised by the people. (Ps 22:6)

5. Then I said to them, You see the trouble we are in, how Jerusalem lies in ruins with its gates burned. Come, let us build the wall of Jerusalem, that we may no longer suffer derision. (Neh 2:17)

The controlling idea in revulsion is to be left exposed to public ridicule for bareness, nakedness, or weakness—like a woman caught without clothes or a city without walls or, in a contemporary context, like the homeless person suffers exposure, ridicule, and abuse.[6] Notice that Jesus cites several of the above messianic passages himself, as when he cites Psalm 22 from the cross (Mark 15:34).

In these passages, Jesus addresses disciples in a communal, honor and shame culture. The Beatitudes address common themes—poverty, hunger, and mourning—shared by disciples

---

6 Addicts and psychiatric patients may also suffer similar abuse, but their public exposure is less physical and more metaphorical.

driven out of and disinherited by their families and communities (Neyrey 1998, 168–169). The three verbs—revile, persecute, and slander—involve similar social stigma and expulsion themes, only with more intensity.

In our own context, the intensity of the response in being reviled underscores the fundamental nature of our faith decision. Jesus says:

> *And brother will deliver brother over to death, and the father his child, and children will rise against parents and have them put to death. And you will be hated by all for my name's sake. But the one who endures to the end will be saved. (Mark 13:12–13)*[7]

Faith in Christ is not an incremental decision, as if we could approach God by tweaking our Sunday morning schedule, or giving more to the church, or occasionally improving our personal conduct. Faith in God is more like a wise guy renouncing the mafia or a rebel fighter responding to an amnesty program by laying down arms. Laying down arms requires a public ceremony where people on both sides notice. The public ceremony of baptism is celebrated both as sacrament of cleansing (baptism by sprinkling) and as a sacrament of death and rebirth (full immersion baptism) emphasizing the transition to faith.

The intensity of this transition to faith in the early church

---

7 Hellerman (2001, 66) writes: *"Jesus assumes that such a shift of loyalties will result in significant relational fallout."*

is often dismissed as merely an example of unity:

> *And all who believed were together and had all things in common. And they were selling their possessions and belongings and distributing the proceeds to all, as any had need.* (Acts 2:44–45)

While this passage is an example of unity, it is also emblematic of significant stress for the disciples, who would normally share such moments primarily with family. Absent family fellowship, the picture of unity here is like an alliance of street people watching out for one another during the winter in the face of intense deprivation.

Intense persecution marks one as a Christian, which also marks one for salvation (Rev 22:4).

Blessed Lord Jesus,

Place your hedge of protection around me, Lord, for I am confused and afraid. My strength fails me; my body aches; my children are yet lost; and it is night—when jackals run freely and the hyena contends with the lion over much carrion. Have mercy on the children, Lord. Spare me their voices in the night; spare me the weeping of souls forgotten and lost—be they familiar, near, and dear. For the workman cannot save from folly nor tell what ears will not hear. Yet, you God hear our prayers; your blessings blossom beyond measure daily. Since the days of my youth, you have comforted me and given me life and hope and joy—to sing and dance and clap hands for the joy of your salvation which is near. But now, let me rest securely until the new day awaits in morning sun with blessings and hope of rest with you, now and always. In the name of the Father, the Son, and the Holy Spirit, Amen.

Questions
1. In what sense is the Ninth Beatitude emphatic?
2. What makes persecution personal?
3. What makes the word, revile, especially painful?
4. What evidence do we have from scripture that early Christians were driven out of their families and communities?

9.2: Suffering Often Predates Salvation

He will swallow up death forever; and the Lord GOD will wipe away tears from all faces, and the reproach of his people he will take away from all the earth, for the LORD has spoken. (Isa 25:8)

Suffering and salvation are prominently linked in the Books of the Law and the Prophets, where emotional distress often amplified the reproach suffered.

In the Books of the Law, consider the reproach suffered by Rachel who was barren and whose older sister, Leah, had six sons and a daughter:

> *Then God remembered Rachel, and God listened to her and opened her womb. She conceived and bore a son and said, God has taken away my reproach.* (Gen 30:22–23)

Rachel's reproach over her barrenness fueled a bitter rivalry with her sister, Leah (Gen 30:1).[1] Because Rachel was also Jacob's favorite wife, her son, Joseph, soon became Jacob's favorite son, as we read:

> *Now Israel [Jacob] loved Joseph more than any other of his sons, because he was the son of his old age. And he made him a robe of many colors.* (Gen 37:3)

---

1 The theme of women teasing each other viciously over barrenness figures prominently in conflict between Sarah and Hagar (Gen 16:4). It also is important in the story of the birth of the Prophet Samuel. There we read: *"And her rival used to provoke her grievously to irritate her, because the LORD had closed her womb."* (1 Sam 1:6)

Jacob's gift of the robe to Joseph signaled the passing of family leadership and made Joseph's half-brothers so jealous that they sold him into slavery in Egypt. They later told Jacob that Joseph had been killed by wild animals (Gen 37).

After suffering at the hands his brothers, being sold into slavery, and sent to prison, Joseph proved himself to be an honest man, a hard worker, and an able leader, but it was God's gift of interpeting dreams that brought him before Pharaoh and led to his promotion to prime minister. As prime minister, Joseph saved Egypt and his own family from starvation during a seven-year famine (Gen 38–45), even though he started out as the son who suffered revulsion and persecution within his family.

In the Books of the Prophets, suffering and persecution are major themes in the story of Job. Job is a righteous man persecuted by Satan (Job 1–2) but reviled by his friends who doubt his righteousness.

One of Job's friends, Eliphaz the Temanite, inquires of Job saying: *"who that was innocent ever perished? Or where were the upright cut off?"* (Job 4:7) Another friend, Bildad the Shuhite, calls Job a windbag and asks: *"Does God pervert justice? Or does the Almighty pervert the right?"* (Job 8:3) This reproach by Job's friends gets so bad that God himself gets angry at these friends and corrects their theological misconceptions saying: *"For you have not spoken of me what is right, as my servant Job has."* (Job 42:7)

In spite of the reproach of his friends and the loss of his family and fortune, God comes to Job's rescue and rewards Job's faithfulness, as we read:

> *And the LORD restored the fortunes of Job, when he had prayed for his friends. And the LORD gave Job twice as much as he had before.* (Job 42:10)

The story of Job highlights the reproach and suffering which are explained in three separate Old Testament ethical approaches.

The first ethical approach is that one is made righteous in keeping the law and unrighteous in breaking it. God enforces the law by rewarding the righteous and punishing the unrighteous, as is the expectation of Job's friend, Eliphaz the Temanite (Job 4:7).[2]

The second approach is that one becomes righteous by gaining wisdom as to how the world really works, as we read: *"One who is wise is cautious and turns away from evil, but a fool is reckless and careless."* (Prov 14:16) In effect, evil is not just bad, it is also stupid, as we often read in Proverbs.

The third approach is that God honors righteous suffer-

---

2 This ethic is outlined in detail in Psalm 1.

ing, as we saw in the life of Job and as we also experience in daily life as deferred gratification. In education, for example, we put off taking a job, study hard, and are typically blessed later with a better job, although the risk of failure is always possible. Still, God rewards those who trust in him and take risks for the kingdom, and punish those who refuse to (Matt 25:14–30).

In God's kingdom, the cross we bear always precedes the crown we wear.

Almighty God,

In our youth, you gave us the law so that our feet would not stumble. In our mid-life journey where scholars offer knowledge and computers offer information, you offer us wisdom. In our seniority you rewarded our sacrifices, giving our vineyard and trees great fruit. We praise you and give you the glory. You have swallowed up death forever, wiped away our tears, and set our feet on solid ground setting straight the reproach of our enemies (Isa 25:8). We praise you and give you the glory. Remember now your church in the storms of deprivation, national strife, and scandalous trials. Give your people eyes that see, ears that hear, and leaders that lead where you would have us go. Bless us with your conspicuous presence by the power of your Holy Spirit and in Jesus' name, Amen.

Questions
1. How does the Old Testament link suffering to salvation?
2. Why does the story of Joseph stand out as an example of suffering and salvation?
3. Can a Christian, like Job, suffer demonic persecution?
4. What three types of righteous are found in the Old Testament?
5. Why is righteous suffering especially insightful?

9.3: Persecution Can Be Transformative

And Saul approved of his [Stephen's] execution. And there arose on that day a great persecution against the church in Jerusalem, and they were all scattered throughout the regions of Judea and Samaria, except the apostles. (Acts 8:1)

*I*n my grandparents' home, every meal began with prayer and ended with a scripture reading. At one point in my college years when I visited and it was my turn to pick a scripture passage, I read a story close to my heart, the story of Stephen:

> *This man never ceases to speak words against this holy place and the law, for we have heard him say that this Jesus of Nazareth will destroy this place and will change the customs that Moses delivered to us.* (Acts 6:13–14)

Stephen offered no defense, but rather he accused the Jews of false worship and not keeping the law (Acts 7:48, 53). Then, he reminded them of Jesus' words during his trial:

> *But I tell you, from now on you will see the Son of Man seated at the right hand of Power and coming on the clouds of heaven.* (Matt 26:64)[1]

Here Jesus paraphrased Daniel 7:13 in a clear claim of divinity. This claim drove the Sanhedrin crazy and in a fit of rage they stoned Stephen, an act illegal under Roman law (John 18:31).

With the execution of Stephen, the Book of Acts introduces Saul (Acts 7:58) who, not only approved of Stephen's

1 Also see: Mark 14:62 and Luke 22:69.

stoning, but led the persecution of Christians in Jerusalem that followed, ravaging the church (λυμαίνω; Acts 8:1, 3). The word, ravage, suggests a self-destructive manner, as in the proverb: *"When a man's folly brings his way to ruin, his heart rages against the LORD."* (Prov 19:3) This manner of persecution confirms Saul's own testimony that he was a zealous persecutor (Acts 8:1; Phil 3:6).

In leading the persecution of the church, Saul assists in scattering the Jerusalem disciples to both the regions of Judea and Samaria—fulfilling the first two parts of the commission of Christ in Acts 1:8, aided by disciples shared the Gospel as they fled Jerusalem (Acts 8:4). Thus, even at his worst Saul acts as an unwilling, unknowing instrument of the Holy Spirit.[2]

When Saul sets out to oppose the third part of Christ's commission in the scattering by going to Damascus, however, the risen Christ intervenes, preventing him from further self-destruction, saying: *"Saul, Saul, why are you persecuting me?"* (Acts 9:4).[3] To this question, Saul responds:

> *Who are you, Lord? And he said, I am Jesus, whom you are persecuting. But rise and enter the city, and you will be told what you are to do.* (Acts 9:5–6)

---

2 Paul directly contributes to the accomplishment of Jesus' charge in Acts 1.8, as cited earlier.

3 This is in stark contrast with the case of Judas Iscariot who ends up committing suicide (Matt 27:5),

Even before he was even aware, the Apostle Paul, formerly Saul, served God's purposes even in persecuting the church and, in doing so, was driven painfully towards his own conversion and call (Acts 9:15–16).

Persecution often traumatizes us, which leaves a mark on us longer than most other things. On an individual level, this trauma can lead to lifelong emotional and psychiatric issues, and, if we then turn into our pain and away from God, can be intensified by spiritual confusion.[4] On a communal level, persecution can be followed by a cycle of revenge between warring communities. At either level, those persecuted and those persecuting are bound in an indelible, negative bond that is not easily broken.

Forgiveness breaks the bond created by abuse and persecution, and makes room for God's Holy Spirit to work in our lives (Rom 12:19). Stephen died praying to God for the forgiveness of his persecutors: *"Lord, do not hold this sin against them."* (Acts 7:60), paraphrasing Christ's own words from the cross (Luke 23:34). As one of those persecutors, Paul never forgot Stephen and mentioned him as he recounted his own conversion before the Sanhedrin—was Paul's conversion God's answer to Stephen's prayer? (Acts 22:20).

---

4 Jesus' prayer at Gethsemane gives us a clear template for dealing with pain in turning to God, not away from him (Matt 26:39–44).

Another important consequence of the Jerusalem persecution was that the Holy Spirit worked to establish the first gentile church in Antioch, as we read:

> Now those who were scattered because of the persecution that arose over Stephen traveled as far as Phoenicia and Cyprus and Antioch, speaking the word to no one except Jews. But there were some of them, men of Cyprus and Cyrene, who on coming to Antioch spoke to the Hellenists also, preaching the Lord Jesus. And the hand of the Lord was with them, and a great number who believed turned to the Lord. (Acts 11:19–21)

The key word here is scattered (διασπαρέντες; "diasparentes") which only appears one other place, in Acts 8:4: "Now those who were scattered [by Saul's persecution] went about preaching the word." The word, scattered, infers an action of the wind[5] and the word for wind in the Greek is pneuma (πνεῦμα), which also translates as Holy Spirit. The inference is that the Holy Spirit established the church at Antioch in response to persecution (Acts 11:22).

Because the apostles remained in Jerusalem at this point, the Holy Spirit used ordinary disciples, whose names remain unknown, to establish the Antioch Church and churches throughout "all Judea and Samaria, and to the end of the earth" (Acts 1:8), much like God has used Pentecostal evangelists in our own time

5 The allusion here is to Luke 8:5–15, *The Parable of the Sower.*

to reach much of the known world.[6] And in many places around the world, persecution remains ever present.

Almighty and Compassionate Father,

The Bible says that through the power of the Holy Spirit, we are to become witnesses to our neighbors, the region, and to the whole world (Acts 1:8). Convict us, Lord, that our witness reaches all in need.

The Bible says that Saul approved of Stephen's execution and afterwards a great persecution arose (Acts 8:1). And that many churches were founded as the disciples were scattered by the Holy Spirit (Acts 11:19). And even the grand persecutor himself, Saul of Tarsus, was himself transformed into an evangelist who we know as Paul (Acts 9:5). Convict us, Lord, that our witness reaches all in need.

Grant us the mind of Christ, we might focus on your priorities, not our own. Transform our hearts that we might feel the things

6 According to statistics published on the number of Christians worldwide, over the last century (1900 to 2000) the number of Christians has increased from roughly 0.5 to 2.0 billion people. During this same period, the share of Christians considered Pentecostal or charismatic has increased from about 0.2 to 23 percent of all Christians (under a million to just under half a billion people). Most of this growth has been in Africa, Asia, and Latin America (IBMR 2015, 29).

that you feel, not feelings of our own. That on the Day of Judgment, we will be judged according to Christ's righteousness, not our own. In the power of your Holy Spirit, give us eyes that see and ears that hear and feet that obey. In Jesus' precious name, Amen.

Questions

1. Do you have a scripture passage that is especially meaningful?

2. What were the charges against Stephen in Acts 6? Did Stephen respond to these charges? Why or why not? Was Stephen's stoning legal?

3. Paul says that he was a zealous persecutor. What evidence supports that conclusion?

4. When Jesus appears to Saul in Acts 9:4, what does he say? Was Paul's persecution personal?

5. What is the significance of the word scattered in Acts 11:19? Who founded the church at Antioch?

6. What was Saul's role in forming the church both before and after his conversion?

9.4: Persecution and Lethargy

But even if you should suffer for righteousness' sake, you will be blessed. Have no fear of them, nor be troubled, but in your hearts honor Christ the Lord as holy, always being prepared to make a defense to anyone who asks you for a reason for the hope that is in you; yet do it with gentleness and respect... (1 Pet 3:14–15)

*B*eing reviled is painful and triggers a Gethsemane moment with a choice—do we turn upward to God or inward into our pain? When we turn to God, our spiritual life blossoms and the church grows; but when we turn to our pain, individually or corporately, then our spiritual life suffers terribly because being reviled is seldom an isolated, one-time event.

Persecution in the modern and postmodern eras has taken on a whole new level of sophistication. The open slander of the Christian faith perpetrated by Marx, Freud, and Nietzsche[1] in the nineteenth century placed church leaders on the philosophical defensive throughout the twentieth century. More recently, the media and other large corporations have actively promoted lifestyles inconsistent with the Christian faith[2] and caused internal questioning of the faith among believers. What greater suf-

1 Slander is an unsubstantiated truth claim designed to deceive or discredit. Plantinga (2000, 167) observes: *"What we saw that this complaint is really the claim that Christian and other theistic belief is irrational in the sense that it originates in cognitive malfunction (Marx) or in cognitive proper function that is aimed at something other than the truth (Freud)."*
2 Allowing malls and other stores to be open on Sunday is probably the most insidious change, but it is seldom the change cited.

fering could a parent experience, for example, then to see their children fall away from the faith and fall into every manner of sin and deprivation? Today's lions may appear only on television, but they are perfectly capable of consuming our faith.

This persistent, low-grade persecution can result in spiritual lethargy which affects all three movements of the spirit—within us, with God, and with others—falling at the lower end of Nouwen's polarities. These can be described as loneliness (within us), illusion (with God), and hostility (with others).[3] Let us turn briefly to examine each of these aspects of spiritual lethargy, starting with loneliness.

Loneliness. Evangelist Charles Finney (1982, 74–76) cited six consequences of squelching the Holy Spirit in our lives:

> *1. Darkness of mind—the truth makes no useful impression,*
>
> *2. Coldness towards religion,*
>
> *3. Holding various errors in religion,*
>
> *4. Disbelief,*
>
> *5. Delusion regarding one's spiritual state, and*
>
> *6. Attempts to justify wrongdoing.*

Cited on this list are each of the tensions—with ourselves (1, 2,

3 An alternative, more secular description might be anxiety/depression/suicide, disbelief, and conflict within the church and society.

3, 5), with God (4), and with others (6)—suggesting different aspects of spiritual lethargy and fertile ground for church conflict.

Illusion. Allusions to persecution fill the New Testament, but they are frequently left out in public readings of scripture leaving the impression that the postmodern church no longer faces persecution[4] and that sin is not intrinsic to the human condition, not part of the context of daily life. Lacking a basic awareness of persecution and sin, the postmodern church struggles less with the emerging persecution evident in our culture and more with the residual context of spiritual lethargy of past decades.

An important indicator of spiritual lethargy suggested by Nouwen is a lack of interest in prayer. Prayer is difficult in the absence of faith which is obvious when the words spoken take precedence over the relationship that we have with God. In the absence of a relationship with God, prayer seems like happy thoughts or a type of poetic expression rather communication with a close friend, confidant, mentor, or father. When we are in relationship with God, our prayers are structured, in part, by

4 The annual number of Christian martyrs in 2015 has been estimated to have been 90,000 people. This is a decline from 377,000 in 1970s in the heyday of world communism, but still about three times the number (34,400) in 1900 (IBMR 2015, 29). Communism is an atheist philosophy and remains widely influential in secular circles even today. Over time, communist nations have been fairly open in their persecution of Christians who are often accused of representing a foreign influence.

the nature of that relationship—a kind of personal theology or spirituality.

Another indicator of spiritual lethargy is the tendency to read scripture out of context or in view of our own personal agendas. One passage often cited out of context is: *"always be[ing] prepared to make a defense to anyone who asks you for a reason for the hope that is in you"* (1 Pet 3:15). This hopeful snippet is often used to argue apologetically for the faith, but contains three important weaknesses. The first weakness is that the snippet ignores the context of persecution, an important reason that First Peter is one of the favorite books of persecuted churches (McKnight 1996, 35). The second weakness is that Peter's admonition to speak *"with gentleness and respect"* is frequently glossed over by apologists anxious for debate. The final weakness is that the focus on offering a verbal defense ignores the Apostle Peter's own emphasis which was on *"lifestyle evangelism"*—living out the faith. Consequently, highlighting only 1 Peter 3:15, which mentions offering a verbal defense of the Gospel, distorts the appeal, attitude, and main point of Peter's letter, which is to inform Christian life in a world of persecution.

Hostility. In a world of persecution, we expect conflict with others over our faith because of the work and power of the

Holy Spirit, as we read:

> *But you will receive power when the Holy Spirit has come upon you, and you will be my witnesses in Jerusalem and in all Judea and Samaria, and to the end of the earth.* (Acts 1:8)

The power of the Holy Spirit normally acts in us to become witnesses, unless we give in to fear and squelch the Holy Spirit's work in our lives.

Fear of taking risks can squelch the power of the Holy Spirit in our lives, as Barthel and Edling (2012, 101) note:

> *When individuals in groups are motivated by fear of the opinion of other people (what others personally think about them) more than the fear of God, their hearts grow cold to the Spirit of God. Lacking God-consciousness, there is no restraining the motivation of the heart; only world passions and popularity with the crowd control. This is common in church conflicts. Defensiveness, self-righteousness, and pride rule the day when people give in to the fear of man.*

While we frequently pray for protection—evidence of fear, the early church prayed for boldness in their witness.[5]

Spiritual lethargy, the opposite of boldness, can also quench the power of the Holy Spirit, as Apostle John observed in

5 *And now, Lord, look upon their threats and grant to your servants to continue to speak your word with all boldness, while you stretch out your hand to heal, and signs and wonders are performed through the name of your holy servant Jesus. And when they had prayed, the place in which they were gathered together was shaken, and they were all filled with the Holy Spirit and continued to speak the word of God with boldness.* (Acts 4:29–31)

the church of Laodicea:

> *I know your works: you are neither cold nor hot.*
> *Would that you were either cold or hot! So, because*
> *you are lukewarm, and neither hot nor cold, I will*
> *spit you out of my mouth.* (Rev 3:15–16)

Spiritual lethargy is widely viewed as a postmodern problem where evangelism is neglected, churches battle over music and decorations, and biblical illiteracy is a problem even among aspiring seminary students.

Church conflicts start with inattention to God's priorities, a corporate dimension of spiritual lethargy. Barthel and Edling (2012, 89) observe churches in conflict coming to their senses when leaders are reminded of the need to remain God-centered and to reframe conflict around well-chosen questions for reflection. Centering worship and our spiritual formation around Christ is therefore an important starting point in reducing and averting church conflict, because the underlying problem is spiritual, not the conflict itself.

The good news about spiritual lethargy is that God is sovereign and the Holy Spirit works in our hearts and minds of Christians everywhere to bring about spiritual revival, as God promised the people of Israel (Deut 30:2–3) and the Apostle Peter preached, citing the Prophet Joel,[6] on the day of Pentecost:

6 (Joel 2:28–29)

And in the last days it shall be, God declares, that I will pour out my Spirit on all flesh, and your sons and your daughters shall prophesy, and your young men shall see visions, and your old men shall dream dreams; even on my male servants and female servants in those days I will pour out my Spirit, and they shall prophesy. (Acts 2:17–18)

While some have become hamstrung with fruitless activities, others have been empowered through Christ's Holy Spirit to work for the reconciliation of the world with Himself (2 Cor 5:17–20).

Lord Most High,

Forgive us for sins known and unknown, transgressions flaunted, and iniquities seen and unseen. Give us penitent hearts that repent, make amends, and seek justice, not just quiet absolution. Transform our lives, Oh Lord, that we might become fit stewards of grace. Let us put on the full righteousness of Christ as knights suiting up for battle that we might extend your kingdom into hearts yet unrepentant and minds shielded from grace. May our lives always speak louder than our words and our words speak only of you. Not squelching your Holy Spirit, but giving your spirit full reign centered on you and you alone. In Jesus' name,

Amen.

Questions

1. What form of denial is often practiced in reading scripture? Why?
2. How many Christians are estimated to have been martyred in 2015? (see footnote)
3. What three things are often missing when 1 Peter 3:15 is cited?
4. Who leads us to become witnesses? What are not reasons that we become witnesses?
5. How does fear work to squelch the Holy Spirit?
6. What church in the Book of Revelations (Rev 3:15–16) was accused of spiritual lethargy?
7. What six consequences of squelching the Holy Spirit does Finney cite?
8. What is the effect of centering on God in church experiencing conflict according to Barthel and Edling?

CONCLUSIONS

Surprising Priorities

Spiritual Links and Tensions

The Road Ahead

Surprising Priorities

For we do not have a high priest who is unable to sympathize with our weaknesses, but one who in every respect has been tempted as we are, yet without sin. (Heb 4:15)

When Christ enters our lives, we begin the journey from our natural selves to the person that God created us to be. This journey transforms our self-image, our faith, and our relationships as we exchange acts of the flesh for fruits of the spirit (Gal 5:19–23). These transformations can be joyful as we grow in personal knowledge, in faith and in relationships; they can also involve painful losses because fundamental change is inherently difficult and losses must be individually grieved.

The change required in the journey of faith is often compared in the Bible with the challenges in marriage.[1] The newly wed is almost always joyous at the initiation of marriage. Yet, the journey from me to we in the first years of marriage can also be challenging because old relationships with our parents, siblings, and spouses must transform into new ones.

The joys and challenges of marriage over those first few years inform the tensions we experience within ourselves, with God, and with others over a lifetime. The first three Beatitudes focus on tension with one's self (humility, mourning, and meek-

---

1 For example, see: Matt 9:15.

ness). The second three Beatitudes focus on tension with God (zeal, mercy, and holiness). The last three Beatitudes focus on tension with others (peacemaking, persecution, and being reviled).

What is most striking about the Beatitudes is that they reveal that Jesus honors humility, mourning, mercy, and peacemaking much more than we do.

Jesus honors the poor in spirit, the humble, which does not come naturally to us. We prefer naturally to build physical strength, self-esteem, assertiveness, and influence over others. Only through the power of the Holy Spirit are we able to grow in humility and to see it mature into the character trait of meekness.

Jesus honors mourning. We do not naturally mourn over the sin in our lives and mourning is the only emotion among the Beatitudes. Other emotions are closer to our hearts and we seek comfort, not transformation. Yet, it is when we pour out our hearts in mourning that we turn to God. This may be why the Apostle Paul admonishes us to: *"rejoice with those who rejoice, [and] weep with those who weep."* (Rom 12:15)

Jesus honors mercy. Mercy is one of God's core values (Exod 34:6) and it lies at the heart of Christ's atoning work on the cross—we see God's love primarily through the lens of His mercy. Mercy is hard for us to ask for and even harder to give which is why we see the hand of God at work in the simple act of forgiveness.

Jesus honors peacemaking—shalom. Shalom forces us to step outside our comfort zone perhaps more than any other Beatitude because by extending peace in all of our relationships we deny ourselves and emulate Christ. Peacemakers must abdicate their privileges, take up the cross daily, dwell in solidarity with all people, and practice sacrificial hospitality.

Jesus' priorities are clearly not our own and they explain Jesus' focus on our transformation, not just in the next life, but in this one. HOW WE LIVE AND HOW WE DIE MATTERS IN THE KINGDOM OF GOD. We know this, not only because of Jesus' life, death, and resurrection (Phil 3:10–11), but also because Stephen and ten of the twelve apostles followed Jesus' example and became martyrs for the faith.

Jesus' example poses a paradox when he admonishes us to treat persecution as a teachable and redemptive moment: *"love your enemies and pray for those who persecute you."* (Matt 5:44). The power of love is revealed when it is unexpected and unearned. We see this power in Christ's words on the cross: *"Father, forgive them, for they know not what they do."* (Luke 23:34)

It is through Christ's atoning sacrifice on the cross that we are reconciled with God and experience the depths of his love.

Jesus' priorities are not naturally our own, but he admonishes us to embrace the Beatitudes and the creative tension that they engender.

Heavenly Father,

We praise you for your gift of salvation available to us through the death and resurrection of Jesus Christ, who, as our great high priest, transcends our weakness having been tempted as we are yet without sin (Heb 4:15) For out of Him, by means of Him, and into Him are all things created, sustained, and restored (Rom 11:36), for which we are grateful. In the power of your Holy Spirit, work in us to complete our journey from isolation in our natural selves to the person that we were created to be, from isolation from others to persons able to offer hospitality to others, and from isolation from God to people of faith. In the power of your Holy Spirit, enable us to follow the example of Jesus Christ who in life, in death, and in resurrection was merciful and gracious, slow to anger, and abounding in steadfast love and faithfulness

(Exod 34:6), even during persecution. In Jesus' name, Amen.

Questions
1. What elements of transformation occur when Christ enters our lives? (Hint: Gal 5:19–23)
2. What is the template for our journey of faith?
3. What three tensions are found in our journey of faith and in the Beatitudes?
4. What surprises do we find in Jesus' priorities as expressed in the Beatitudes?
5. What is surprising about Jesus' attitude about persecution?
6. What is the Christian paradox?

Spiritual Links and Tensions

Do not think that I have come to abolish the Law or the Prophets; I have not come to abolish them but to fulfill them. (Matt 5:17)

*T*he subjective tensions in our spiritual life track the objective gaps in our inward, upward, and outward relationships, and are deeply rooted in the witness of the Old Testament. In the inward gap, which arises between who we were and the person that God created us to be, we find allusions to the person of Moses. In the upward gap, which arises between us and God, we find allusions to the character of God Himself. In the outward gap, which arises between us and those around us, we find allusions to the messianic prophecies of Isaiah. Together, these gaps and tensions suggest how Jesus intended Old Testament prophecy to be fulfilled.

Focusing on the inward gap, the first three Beatitudes:

> *Honored are the poor in spirit, for theirs is the kingdom of heaven. Honored are those who mourn, for they shall be comforted. Honored are the meek, for they shall inherit the earth.* (Matt 5:3–5)

These Beatitudes focus on who we are and borrow their language, in part, from Isaiah 61:1 but the influence goes further back to the attitude and person of Moses, as in: "*Now the man Moses was very meek, more than all people who were on the face of the earth.*" (Num 12:3). The dominant motif in these three Beatitudes—meekness or humility—is expressed by Moses whose overall spirituality is well-defined in the Books of the Law.

Focusing on the upward gap, the second three Beatitudes:

> *Honored are those who hunger and thirst for righteousness, for they shall be satisfied. Honored are the merciful, for they shall receive mercy. Honored are the pure in heart, for they shall see God.* (Matt 5:6–8)

These Beaitudes focus on God and God's core values expressed in Exodus 34:6:

> *The LORD passed before him and proclaimed, The LORD, the LORD, a God merciful and gracious, slow to anger, and abounding in steadfast love and faithfulness* (Exod 34:6).

The repeated references to God's character in the Old Testament, especially Jonah 4:2, highlight God's mercy and Christ's atoning work on the cross (1 Cor 15:3).

Focusing on the outward gap, the last three Beatitudes:

> *Honored are the peacemakers, for they shall be called sons of God. Honored are those who are persecuted for righteousness' sake, for theirs is the kingdom of heaven. Honored are you when others revile you and persecute you and utter all kinds of evil against you falsely on my account.* (Matt 5:9–11)

These Beatitudes focus on what we do and draw us back to Isaiah

61:1:

> *The Spirit of the Lord GOD is upon me, because the LORD has anointed me to bring good news to the poor; he has sent me to bind up the brokenhearted, to proclaim liberty to the captives, and the opening of the prison to those who are bound;* (Isa 61:1)

God's sovereign work instituting shalom in a social context is unexpected—we do not expect to experience God's presence in the context of persecution.[1] Yet, even during persecution God is not only present, he is sovereignly at work to transform lives and to offer shalom, the heart of Christian spirituality.

The Beatitudes are a key to Jesus' own spirituality. A complete spirituality needs to answer four important questions (Kreeft 2007, 6)[2] The Beatitudes answer three of these four questions: who are we? (we are meek like Moses); who is God? (God is merciful . . .); and what do we do about it? (we offer shalom). Jesus' resurrection answers the fourth question: how do we know? (because Christ rose from the dead).

Knowing that the Beatitudes are anchored in the Old Testament, not only highlights God's immutable character traits in Exodus 34:6, it ties Christ's divinity to them. The Beatitudes

---

1 The word associations in this passage are actually stronger with the first three Beatitudes.

2 These questions are often associated with related fields of study: metaphysics (study of God), anthropology (study of humanity), ethics (study of right and wrong actions), and epistemology (study of knowledge).

and their scriptural context assure that we do not shape Jesus into a likeness of our own image. This is why the early church focused intensely on the Beatitudes[3] and why the Beatitudes deserve special study today.

Heavenly Father,

We praise you for the gift of your Holy Spirit to guide our thoughts and protect our hearts that we might grow more humble in each passing day. We praise you for the example of Jesus of Nazareth who extended us shalom in the midst of the chaos of our lives that we might extend shalom to those around us. We praise you for your example of holiness that we might hunger and thirst for no one but you. We confess that our hearts and minds are corrupted with the sin of this world; cleanse us through the blood of the Lamb. In Jesus' precious name, Amen.

---

3 Guelich (1982, 14) citing Kissinger (1975) reports that: *"Matthew 5–7 [appears] more frequently than any other three chapters in the entire Bible in the Ante Nicene [early church] writings".*

Questions
1. What are the three movements in our spiritual life?
2. What are three important scripture passages influencing the Beatitudes?
3. What are the four big questions of philosophy?
4. Why does it matter that the Beatitudes are well-grounded in scripture?

The Road Ahead

that I may know him and the power of his resurrection, and may share his sufferings, becoming like him in his death, that by any means possible I may attain the resurrection from the dead. (Phil 3:10–11)

*I*n the Beatitudes Jesus teaches his disciples a simple lesson: HOW WE LIVE AND HOW WE DIE MATTERS IN THE KINGDOM OF GOD. This kingdom principle is borne out as we reduce tension with ourselves, with God, and with other people in each of the three movements of our spiritual lives. But our journey in life is not random, we know that in life, death, and resurrection the future is in Christ.

In Christ, we look beyond our natural selves to the person that God created us to be. In our natural selves, we scoff at the idea of living sacrificially without aspiring for personal gain or glory. In our natural selves, we think of holiness as being other worldly and mysterious. In our natural selves hope is futile and death has the final claim. But now we live, not in our natural selves, but in Christ.

In Christ, we live relieved of our obsession with past failures and present circumstances, chains that have been broken. Because our identity is in Christ and not in circumstances, our identity is secure in the immutable character of Christ, not evolving with changes in fashion, law, or science. Because our identity is in Christ and Christ sacrificed himself for us, we too can live sacrificially and be more fully present in our family life, church life, and work in the world, even loving our enemies. In Christ, we are truly a new creation.

In Christ even in death we can count the cost of discipleship knowing our future is secure (1 Pet 1:3) in spite of failing health, persecution, rejection, and even death. Wherever life takes us we never leave the sovereign dominion of Christ and the shalom of God goes with us,[1] as the Apostle Paul writes:

> *For I am sure that neither death nor life, nor angels nor rulers, nor things present nor things to come, nor powers, nor height nor depth, nor anything else in all creation, will be able to separate us from the love of God in Christ Jesus our Lord.* (Rom 8:38–39)

BECAUSE JESUS ROSE FROM THE DEAD, these words are trustworthy and give meaning to life allowing us to live fearlessly in joy, not being confined to our old nature.

In Christ, the hope of the resurrection means that our attitude in life and death is different, because living in the image of our creator and expecting both persecution and death, we await the glory of Christ in our resurrection (Phil 3:10–12). An-

---

1 *"Simon Peter answered him, Lord, to whom shall we go? You have the words of eternal life, and we have believed, and have come to know, that you are the Holy One of God."* (John 6:68–69)

ticipating these events, the hope of the resurrection serves both as a road-map and as a source of energy. In Christ, we are a new creation equipped with an objective, a map, and the strength to pursue our daily journey.

In this journey, humility nurtures our Christian authenticity, as we become God's living artwork in creation,[2] and marks us as Christians, from heart to mind—like an onion, which is consistent from core to skin and back again.

So our faith is in Christ and, like Paul, we emulate Christ's life and death so that somehow we might attain the resurrection and eternal life (Phil 3:10–12).

Holy and Eternal Father,

Draw me to yourself—open my heart, illumine my mind, and strengthen my hands in your service. Let me follow the example of Jesus Christ, who lived as a role model for sinners, died on the cross to atone for our sins, and who rose from the dead to give us the hope of glory. Through the power of the Holy Spirit, bridge

---

2 In writing about the contribution of art to spirituality, Dyrness (2001, 101) observes: *"How does art relate to this program of God? Human art, when it is good, manages some echo of this [God's] reality."*

any gap and resolve any tension that hinders my sanctification, blocks ministry to those around me, or blinds me to your call on my life. Grant me a faith that transcends both lethargy and suffering that I might live and die as your witness through the power of your Holy Spirit and covered by the blood of the Lamb. In Jesus' precious name, Amen.

Questions
1. What is a lesson that Jesus teaches?
2. What are the three movements of the spirit?
3. What onion characteristic informs our Christian journey?
4. What is our source of authenticity and strength?
5. What does the expression, in Christ, mean? What is its antithesis?

REFERENCES

Baker, David W. 2006. *The NIV Application Commentary: Joel, Obadiah, and Malachi*. Grand Rapidss: Zondervan.

Baker, Kenneth [Editor]. 1995. *The NIV Study Bible*. Grand Rapids: Zondervan.

Barthel, Tara Klena and David V. Edling. 2012. *Redeeming Church Conflicts: Turning Crisis into Compassion and Care*. Grand Rapids: BakerBooks.

Bauer, Walter (BDAG). 2000. *A Greek-English Lexicon of the New Testament and Other Early Christian Literature*. 3rd ed. ed. de Frederick W. Danker. Chicago: University of Chicago Press. <BibleWorks. v .9.>.

Benner, David G. 1998. *Care of Souls: Revisioning Christian Nurture and Counsel*. Grand Rapids: Baker Books.

Bethune, George. 1839. *The Fruit of the Spirit*. Reiner Publications.

BibleWorks. 2015. *Norfolk, VA: BibleWorks, LLC*. <BibleWorks v.10>.

Bivin, David and Roy Blizzard. 1994. *Understanding the Difficult Words of Jesus: New Insights from a Hebraic Perspective*. Shippensburg, PA: Destiny Image Publishers.

Blackaby, Richard. 2012. *The Seasons of God: How the Shifting Patterns of Your Life Reveal His Purposes for You*. Colorado Springs: Multnomah Books.

Bonhoeffer, Dietrich. 1995. *The Cost of Discipleship (Orig.* pub. 1937). New York: Simon and Schuster.

Bridges, Jerry. 1996a. *The Practice of Godliness*. Colorado Springs: NavPress.

Bridges, Jerry. 1996b. *The Pursuit of Holiness*. Colorado Springs: NavPress.

Brown-Driver-Briggs-Gesenius (BDB). 1905. *Hebrew-English Lexicon, unabridged*.

Brueggemann, Walter. 2014. *Sabbath as Resistance: Saying NO to the Culture of Now*. Louisville: Westminster John Knox Press.

Card, Michael. 2005. *A Sacred Sorrow Experience Guide: Reaching Out to God in the Lost Language of Lament*. Colorado Springs: NavPress.

Cloud, Henry and John Townsend. 1992. *Boundaries: When to Say YES, When to Say NO, To Take Control of Your Life*. Grand Rapids: Zondervan.

Colson, Charles and Harold Pickett. 2005. *The Good Life*. Carol Stream: Tyndale House Publishers.

Crawford, Evans E. and Thomas H. Troeger. 1995. *The Hum: Call and Response in African American Preaching.* Nashville: Abingdon Press.

Dayton, Donald W. 2005. *Discovering An Evangelical Heritage.* Peabody: Hendrickson.

Dyrness,William A. 2001. *Visual Faith: Art, Theology, and Worship in Dialogue.* Grand Rapids: Baker Academic.

Elliott, Matthew A. 2006. *Faithful Feelings: Rethinking Emotion in the New Testament.* Grand Rapids, MI: Kregel.

Ellis, Ralph and Ed Payne. 2015. *"Kim Davis asks Kentucky governor to free her in same-sex marriage case".* CNN.Cited: 7 September 2015. Online: http://www.cnn.com/2015/09/07/politics/kim-davis-same-sex-marriage-kentucky-governor.

Fairbairn, Donald. 2009. *Life in the Trinity: An Introduction to Theology with the Help of the Church Fathers.* Downers Grove: IVP Academic.

Finney, Charles. 1982. *The Spirit-Filled Life (Orig pub 1845–61).* New Kensington: Whitaker House.

Foxe, John and Harold J. Chadwick. 2001. The New Foxes' Book of Martyrs (Orig Pub 1563). Gainsville, FL: Bridge-Logos Publishers.

France, R.T. *1985*. Matthew. Tyndale New Testament Commentaries. Downers Grove: IVP Academic.

France, R.T. 2007. The Gospel of Matthew. New International Commentary on the New Testament. Grand Rapids: Eerdmans.

Geisler, Norman L. 2007. *A Popular Survey of the Old Testament.* Grand Rapids: BakerBooks.

Graham, Billy. 1955. *The Secret of Happiness.* Garden City, NY: Doubleday and Company, Inc.

Guelich, Robert. 1982. *The Sermon on the Mount: A Foundation for Understanding.* Dallas: Word Publishing.

Haas, Guenther H. 2004. *"Calvin's Ethics."* In The Cambridge Companion to John Calvin, 93–105. Edited by Donald K. McKim. New York: Cambridge University Press.

Hellerman, Joseph H. 2001. *The Ancient Church as Family.* Minneapolis: Fortress Press.

Hernandez, Wil. 2006. *Henri Nouwen: A Spirituality of Imperfection.* New York: Paulist Press.

Hickman, Dave. 2016. *Closer than Close: Awakening to the Freedom of Your Union with Christ.* Colorado Springs: NavPress.

Horton, Michael. 2011. *The Christian Faith: A Systemic Theology for Pilgrims on the Way*. Grand Rapids: Zondervan.

International Bulletin of Missionary Research (IBMR). 2015. *Christianity 2015: Religious Diversity and Personal Contact*. Cited: 28 December 2015. Online: http://www.gordonconwell.edu/ockenga/research/documents/1IBMR2015.pdf. Pages 28–29.

Kinnaman, David with Gabe Lyons. 2007. *UnChristian: What a New Generation Really Thinks About Christianity...and Why It Matters*. Grand Rapids: BakerBooks.

Kissinger, W.S. *1975. The Sermon on the Mount: A History of Interpretation and Bibliography*. ATLA 3. Metuchen: Scarecrow.

Kreeft, Peter. 2007. *The Philosophy of Jesus*. South Bend, IN: Saint Augustine Press.

Ladd, George Eldon. 1991. *A Theology of the New Testament*. Grand Rapids: Eerdmans.

Lester, Andrew D. 2007. *Anger: Discovering Your Spiritual Ally*. Louisville: Westminster John Knox Press.

Lucado, Max. 2012. *Fearless*. Grand Rapids: Zondervan.

McGrath, Alister. 2004. *The Twilight of Atheism*. New York: DoubleDay.

McKnight, Scott. 1992. *"Gospel of Matthew"* pages 526–541 of *Dictionary of Jesus and the Gospels in Compendium of Contemporary Biblical Scholarship*. Edited by Joel B. Green, Scot McKnight, and I. Howard Marshall. Downers Grove: InterVarsity Press.

McKnight, Scott. 1996. *The NIV Application Commentary: 1 Peter*. Grand Rapids: Zondervan.

Metaxas, Eric. 2012. *Bonhoeffer: Pastor, Martyr, Prophet, Spy*. Nashville: Thomas Nelson.

Mitchell, Kenneth R. and Herbert Anderson. *1983*. All Our Losses; All Our Griefs: Resources for Pastoral Care. Louisville: Westminster John Knox Press.

Mouw, Richard J. 2010. *Uncommon Decency: Christian Civility in an Uncivil World*. Downers Grove: InterVarsity Press.

Nestle, Eberhard and Erwin, and Barbara and Kurt Aland (Nestle-Aland). 28th edition. *Novum Testamentum Graece*. Stuttgart: Bibelgesellschaft, 2012.

Neyrey, Jerome H. 1998. *Honor and Shame in the Gospel of Matthew*. Louisville: Westminster John Knox Press.

Niebuhr, Richard. 2001. *Christ and Culture (Orig.* pub. 1951). New York: HarperSanFrancisco.

Noll, Mark A. 2002. *America's God: From Jonathan Edwards to Abraham Lincoln.* New York: Oxford University Press.

Nouwen, Henri J. M. *1975.* Reaching Out: The Three Movements of the Spiritual Life. New York: DoubleDay.

Nouwen, Henri J. M. *1989.* In the Name of Jesus: Reflections on Christian Leadership. New York: Crossroad Publishing Company.

Nouwen, Henri J.M. *2010.* Wounded Healer: Ministry in Contemporary Society (Orig pub 1972). New York: Image Doubleday.

Ortberg, John. 2012. *Who Is This Man? The Unpredictable Impact of the Inescapable Jesus.* Grand Rapids: Zondervan.

Ortberg, John. 2015. *All the Places to Go: How Will You Know? Carol Stream: Tyndale House Publishers.*

Plantinga, Alvin. 2000. *Warranted Christian Belief.* New York: Oxford University Press.

Saslow, Eli , Sarah Kaplan, and Joseph Hoyt. 2015. *"Oregon shooter said to have singled out Christians for killing in horrific act of cowardice"* Published: October 2, 2015. Washington Post. Cited: 29 December 2015. Online: https://www.washingtonpost.com/news/morning-mix/wp/2015/10/02/oregon-shooter-said-to-have-singled-out-christians-for-killing-in-horrific-act-of-cowardice.

Savage, John. 1996. *Listening and Caring Skills: A Guide for Groups and Leaders.* Nashville: Abingdon Press.

Scazzero, Peter. 2006. *Emotionally Healthy Spirituality.* Grand Rapids: Zondervan.

Schnabel, Eckhard J. 2004. *Early Christian Mission.* Vol 1: Jesus and the Twelve. Downers Grove: InterVarsity Press.

Sedler, Michael D. 2003. *When to Speak Up & When to Shut Up: Principles for Conversations You Won't Regret.* Minneapolis: Baker Publishing Group (Chosen).

Smith, Houston. 2001. *Why Religion Matters: The Fate of the Human Spirit in an Age of Disbelief.* San Francisco: Harper.

Smith, James K. A. *2006.* Who's Afraid of Postmodernizm: Taking Derrida, Lyotard, and Foucault to Church. Grand Rapids: Baker Academic.

Spangler, Ann and Lois Tverberg. 2009. *Sitting at the Feet of Rabbi Jesus: How the Jewishness of Jesus Can Transform Your Faith*. Grand Rapids: Zondervan.

Turkle, Sherry. 2011. *Alone Together: Why we Expect More from Technology and Less from Each Other*. New York: Basic Books.

Wallace, Daniel B. 1996. *Greek Grammar Beyond the Basics: An Exegetical Syntax of the New Testament*. Grand Rapids: Zondervan.

White, James Emery. 2004. *Serious Times: Making Your Life Matter in an Urgent Day*. Downers Grove: InterVarsity Press.

Wikipedia. 2015a. *"Charleston church shooting"* [of June 17, 2015]. Cited: 29 December 2015. Online: https://en.wikipedia.org/wiki/Charleston_church_shooting.

Wikipedia. 2015b. *"Demographics of the United States"*. Cited 29 December 2015. Online: https://en.wikipedia.org/wiki/Demographics_of_the_United_States.

Wikipedia. 2015c. *"Presbyterian Church (USA)"*. Cited: 29 December 2015. Online: https://en.wikipedia.org/wiki/Presbyterian_Church_(USA).

Wilkins, Michael J. 2004. *The NIV Application Commentary: Matthew*. Grand Rapids: Zondervan.

Yancey, Philip. 1990. *Where is God When It Hurts*. Grand Rapids: Zondervan.

Younger, K. Lawson. *2002*. The NIV Application Commentary: Judges and Ruth. Grand Rapids: Zondervan.

SCRIPTURAL INDEX

OLD TESTAMENT

Genesis

1:1	41, 147
1:2–4	xii
1:3	83
1:4	84
1:27	118, 136
1:28	100
2:8–10	107
3:3	202
3:6	5
3:8–9	144
3:15	5, 168
3:21	84, 104
3:23	108
3:24	168
4:3–9	193
4:5–7	169
4:6–8	xi
6	115
6:5–6	61
6:5–8	85
6:6	56
6:7–8	61
12:1–3	195
12:2	138, 139
12:2–3	29
12:3	50
13:10	20
16:4	218
18	50
18:2–5	50
18:17–20	19
18:23–32	20
19:16	20
19:26	20
20	50
20:4–6	144
21:22–23	50
23:2	61
25:26–34	173
30:1	218

(Genesis continued)

30:22–23	218
30:23	213
35:18	55
37	219
37:2–28	173
37:3	218
38–45	219
50:3	61

Exodus

1:8	56
1:22	62
2:6	62
2:11–15	174
3:1	196
3:6	143
3:7	196
3:10	196
3:12	197
3:14–15	197
4:21	64
7:16	104
14:28	40
17:1–17	103
17:3	109
20	147, 174
20:2	148, 198
20:3	105
20:16	57
34:4–7	122
34:6	16, 87, 127, 128, 133, 134, 137, 158, 239, 240, 244, 245, 246
34:6–7	127

Leviticus

11:44	ix, 142
20:17	214
23:34–43	103

Numbers

11:10.............................. 62
12:3.............40, 41, 45, 58, 83, 83
12:6–8............................... 40
12:13............................. 62

Deuteronomy

1:20–37............................ 148
3:1................................. 39
4:31.............................. 127
5..................................174
6:4............................... 143
6:4–5............................. 155
6:5............................... 143
6:13.............................. 94
6:16.............................. 94
8:3..............................114, 94
8:11–16........................... 109
11:4.............................. 192
11:13–15......................... 108
18:15............................. 150
28...............................26
28:1–3............................ 148
28:15–16......................... 149
28:47–48......................... 109
30:1–3............................ 174
30:1–3.............................. 63
30:2–3............................ 234

Judges

3:9............................... 63
11:30–40......................... 197
17:6.............................. 62

1 Samuel

1:6.............................. 218
10:1.............................. 152
11:2.............................. 152

2 Samuel

24:21–25........................... 16

1 Kings

12................................ 176
12:14............................. 176
12:26–29.......................... 197
14:16............................. 176

2 Kings

19:36............................. 129
24................................56

2 Chronicles

1:10–13........................... 109
7:14.............................. 50
12:1–2............................ 176

Ezra

1:1–3............................. 56

Nehemiah

2:17.............................. 214

Job

1:1..............................198, 15
1–2.............................199, 219
1:8............................... 199
1:9............................... 149
1:12............................. 15
4:7............................ 219, 220
8:3............................... 219
19:25............................. 199
19:25–27......................... 149
19:26–27.....................143
42:1–7........................... 149
42:7.............................. 220
42:10............................. 220

Psalms

1................... 35, 26, 28, 26, 220
1:1.............................. 149
1:1–2............................ 26
1:1–2............................ 35
2................................ 27
2:11–12.......................... 24
8:2.............................. 34

(Psalms continued)

16:10.................................. 2
22.................................. 214
22:1............................... 96, 103
22:6.............................. 214
22:23.............................. 96
24:1–4.............................. 157
24:3–4.............................. 142
25:6–7.............................. 123
25:9.............................. 86
37:11.............................. 78, 86
42:1–3.............................. 107
51:10–11.........................147, 150
51:10–12........................ 143
86:15........................ 127, 128
89:46.............................. 104
103................................128
103:8.............................. 127
126:5.............................. 61
126:5–6.............................. 69
130.............................. 64
130:1–4.............................. 64
130:4.............................. 64

Proverbs

1:7................................ 109, 149
3:34.................................. 47
14:16.............................. 220
19:3.............................. 224
25:21–22........................ 109

Song of Solomon

2:15.............................. 160

Isaiah

6:5.............................. xi, 57
9:6.............................. 173
9:6–7.............................. 176
11:1–5.............................. 86
11:6.............................. 177
25:8........................214, 218, 221
30..................................27
30:20.............................. 27
36:2.............................. 129

(Isaiah continued)

37:37.............................. 129
40:11.............................. 91
42:1–3.............................. 37
51:1.............................. 207
53.............................. 193
53:11.............................. 192
54:9.............................. 85
55:1–2.............................. 110
61.............................. 35, 41
61:1...... 41, 42, 45, 41, 86, 244, 245
61:1–3............ 35, 41, 180
61:2.............................. 56

Jeremiah

1:15–16.............................. 176
3:15.............................. 110
4:28.............................. 67
6:12–14.............................. 175
8:18–19.............................. 62
29:10–14.............................. 56
29:11.............................. 67
31:15.............................. 55
31:31–34........................ 42, 199

Ezekiel

1:28.............................. 143
2:1.............................. 143, 202
34:2.............................. 58

Daniel

3:23–25.............................. 200
7:13.............................202, 223

Hosea

6:6........................ 123, 124, 132

Joel

2:13.............................127, 128
2:28–29.............................. 234

Jonah

1:2–3	128
3:9–10	129
4:2	127, 128, 129, 244

Nahum

1:1	128

Zechariah

9:9	87
13:9	164

Malachi

3:2	164
3:3	73
3:6	87
4:1	57

NEW TESTAMENT

Matthew

1:18–25	25
2:1–13	25
2:18	55
3:2	57
3:2	37, 50
4	24
4:12	25
4:17	24, 37, 50
4:18–22	24
4:19	25
4:23–25	24
5:1–11	xii
5:3	3, 34, 41
5:3–5	10, 243
5:3–12	24
5:4	54, 58, 59, 61, 64
5:5	58
5:6	102, 119
5:6–8	16, 244
5–7	xiii, 24
5:7	122
5:8	142
5:9	186, 188, 189
5:9–11	21, 244
5:10	192, 200
5:11	212
5:11–12	28
5:12	vi, 206
5:13	44, 208
5:14–16	xii, 44
5:17	vii, 39, 41, 159, 243
5:19–20	37
5:20	37
5:21–24	57
5:21–26	169
5:22	80
5:27–29	152
5:29	152
5:30	152
5:37	80
5:39	203
5:39–41	80

(Matthew continued)

5:41	203
5:43–45	19
5:43–46	115
5:44	21, 194, 203, 240
5:44–45	109
5:44–48	170
6:10	136
6:10–15	137
6:12	124, 136
6:14–15	137, 50
6:15–34	58
6:21	112
6:25	68
6:31–33	105
6:33	58
7:1	203
7:12	124
8:12	56
9:13	124, 132
9:15	55, 238
10	170
10:11–15	21
10:13	170
10:14	21
10:24–25	194
10:34	170, 188
10:35–38	58
10:39	200
10:42	90
11:21	58
11:28–30	9, 10
11:29	78, 87, 90
12:7	124
12:46	58
13:31	37
14:10	25
16:16	v
18:33	124
21:5	79
21:16	34
22:17–22	80
22:21	203
22:36–40	72, 143
23:9	186

(Matthew continued)

23:23	124
23:25	154
23:34–47	˙181
25:14–30	221
25:31–46	104
25:37	114
26:38–39	71
26:39	45, 47
26:39–44	225
26:42–44	47
26:62–63	79
26:64	223
28:5	224

Mark

2:27	65
3	64, 65
3:4–6	64
3:4–6	66
4:30	37
5:15	181
5:20	181
5:38–41	67
6:11	21
9:42	90
9:50	44
13:12–13	215
14:36	47
14:62	223
15:34	96, 214

Luke

4	35
4:1–2	94
4:4	114
4:4, 7, 9	94
4:14–21	179
4:18–19	41
4:31–36	180
4:38	180
4:41	180
5:13–15	67
6	24

(Luke continued)

6:7–11	24
6:13–16	24
6:20	36
6:20, 24	57
6:20–26	24
6:21	69, 72, 102
6:22	212
6:27–25	45
7:11–16	55
7:33–35	144
7:36–50	164
8:5–15	226
9:5	21
9:52–56	20
10:11	21
10:25–28	132
10:25–37	188
10:29	132
10:36	133
10:37	133
13:18	37
14:34	44
17:2	90
21:12–13	203
22:25–26	47
22:42	47
22:69	223
23:34	206, 225, 240
23:39–43	193

John

1:14	128
1:16–17	158
1:41	56
2:1–10	114
2:1–11	102
2:6–10	183
3	37
3:16	19, 169, 182
4:28–30	181
4:32	114
5:19	136
6:5–14	103

(John continued)

6:11	114
6:68–69	249
7:2	103
7:37–39	103
10:11	91
10:11–16	110
11–12	55
11:33–43	67
13:1–3	46
13:3, 4, 14	46
13:4–5	45
13:8–9	46
13:34–35	19
14:6	87
14:27	171
15:2	152
16:7–8	155
18:31	223
20:19–21	179
20:21–22	145
21:3–13	103
21:15	92
21:15–18	92

Acts

1:6–8	49, 51
1:7–8	52
1:8	224, 231, 233
1.8	224
2:14–41	2
2:17–18	235
2:44–45	216
4:29–31	233
6	228
6:13–14	223
7	204
7:48–53	194
7:48, 53	223
7:58	223
7:60	225
8:1	223, 224, 227
8:1, 3	224
8:4	224, 226
9:3	143

(Acts continued)

9:4................................. 224, 228
9:4–5................................. 12
9:5................................. 227
9:5–6................................. 224
9:15–16......................... 14, 225
11:19......................... 227, 228
11:19–21......................... 226
11:19–22............................. 63
11:22............................. 226
13:16–41............................. 2
13:51............................. 21
15:19–20......................... 160
22:6............................. 143
22:20............................. 225
26............................. 143
26:13............................. 143
26:16............................. 143

Romans

1:28............................. 21
5:1............................. 169
5:6–8............................. 213
6:1–2............................. 159
6:19............................. ix
7............................. 15
7:14............................. 148
7:15............................. x, 7
7:18–19......................... 95
8:22............................. 67
8:31............................. 197
8:34–39......................... 207
8:35–37......................... 194
8:38–39......................... 249
10:9............................. 2
11:36............................. 241
12:14......................... 206, 209
12:14–15............................. 67
12:15............................. 239
12:18............................. 182
12:19............................. 225
12:20–21......................... 115

1 Corinthians

1:2................................ix
3:12–13............................. 164
4:10–12............................. 112
6:19............................. 114
9:4............................. 113
9:22............................. 164
15:3......................185, 123, 202
15:3–5............................. 182
15:3–10............................. 150
15:17............................. 13
15:20............................. 155
15:55............................. 96

2 Corinathians

3:16–18................................ix
3:18............................. 32
4:7–10............................. 96
4:12............................. 200
5:17............................. ix, xiii
5:17–20............................. 235
7:10......................... 55, 64, 68
10:1............................. 79
11:7............................. 113
11:23–28......................... 15, 113
12:7............................. 15
12:9............................. 113
12:10–11............................. 112

Galatians

3:13............................. 155
3:27–28......................... 203, 205
5:19–23............32, 83, 91, 238, 242
5:19–24......................... 187, 189
5:22–23............................. 186
5:22–23............................. 137

Ephesians

4:20–24............................. 153
5:32............................. v
6:13–17............................. 156

Philippians

3:6.............................. 149, 224
3:8................................... 14
3:8–9............................... 100
3:10–11..............2, 67, 240, 248
3:10–11............................... 5
3:10–12...................... 249, 250
3:14.................................. 3
3:20............................... 206
4:11–13............................. 48

Colossians

1:24................................. 3
3:12–14............................ 91

1 Thessalonians

4:13................................ 68
5:19................................. x

1 Timothy

4:7................................ 154
6:11............................... 94

2 Timothy

2:20................................. x
2:24–26............................ 91

Hebrews

4:15......................155, 238, 241

James

1:2–3.............................. 200
1:2–4.............................. 192
1:21................................ 79
1:22................................ 10
1:22–25........................... 154
2:13.............................. 133
2:15–16............................ 19
2:23................................ 40
3:13................................ 91
4:6................................. 47
4:8–10............................. 58

1 Peter

1:3.............................. 3, 67
1:3–5............................. 134
2:10–12........................... 207
2:24.............................. 202
3:13–17....................... 79, 208
3:14–15........................... 229
3:15..................... 91, 232, 236
3:16–17........................... 209
4:12.............................. 200
4:16.............................. 193
5:5................................ 47

Revelation

3:15–16......................234, 236
3:20................................. 4
7:17............................91, 94
20:5.............................. 204
21:6.........................115, 116
22:3.............................. 155
22:3–4............................ 144
22:4.............................. 216
22:17............................. 110

ABOUT THE AUTHOR

*A*uthor Stephen W. Hiemstra (MDiv, PhD) is a slave of Christ, husband, father, tentmaker, writer, speaker . . . He lives in Centreville, VA with Maryam, his wife of more than thirty years. Together, they have three grown children.

Stephen has been an active writer throughout his career; both as an economist and as a pastor. As an economist of 27 years working in more than 5 federal agencies, he published numerous government studies, magazine articles, and book reviews. *A Christian Guide to Spirituality* (July 2014) was, however, his first published book. A Spanish edition[1] was published in September 2015.

Stephen is a second career tentmaker who divides his time between Hispanic ministry, blogging with an online pastor theme, and occasional consulting in financial engineering. This online ministry includes Bible studies, book reviews, guest posts, and spiritual reflections. As a hospital chaplain intern, he worked in the emergency department, a psychiatric unit, and an Alzheimer's unit. He is an elder in Centreville Presbyterian Church.

He has a masters of divinity (MDiv, 2013) from Gordon-Conwell Theological Seminary in Charlotte, NC. His doc-

1 *Unia Guía Cristiana a la Espiritualidad*. Details available at: T2Pneuma. com.

torate (PhD, 1985) is in agricultural economics from Michigan State University in East Lansing, MI. Although a U.S. citizen, Stephen studied in Puerto Rico and Germany, and speaks Spanish and German.

Correspond with Stephen at T2Pneuma@gmail.com or follow him on T2Pneuma.net and @T2Pneuma.

AFTERWORD

*T*hank you for taking time to read my book, *Life in Tension*. Researching and writing this book has been a blessing for me and I hope that you have also been blessed. Haven't you always wanted to hear the words of Jesus, to walk in his footsteps, and to experience the joy of salvation? I have.

If you have enjoyed *Life in Tension*, then I encourage you to tell your family and friends. Your can also share with other readers by writing a review and posting it on Amazon. com or in any other forum where reviews can be posted.

Yours in Christ,

Stephen